Kim Izzo is the features editor at *Flare* magazine. She has been a frequent contributor to various newspapers and magazines including *The Globe and Mail* (Canada's national newspaper), *Style* and *Fashion* magazine. Previously she worked as a television producer on series including *Entertainment Tonight* and *Access Hollywood*.

Ceri Marsh is the fashion news director at *Fashion* magazine, and was previously fashion editor at *The Globe and Mail*. Her articles have appeared frequently in magazines such as *Toronto Life* and *Flare*.

Izzo and Marsh currently write a weekly etiquette column for *The Globe and Mail* entitled 'Urban Decorum'.

The Fabulous Girl's Guide to Decorum

Kim Izzo and Ceri Marsh

CORGI BOOKS

THE FABULOUS GIRL'S GUIDE TO DECORUM
A CORGI BOOK : 0 552 14938 1

First publication in Great Britain

PRINTING HISTORY
Corgi edition published 2002
1 3 5 7 9 10 8 6 4 2

Set in Garamond by Falcon Oast Graphic Art Ltd.

Corgi Books are published by Transworld Publishers,
61–63 Uxbridge Road, London W5 5SA,
a division of The Random House Group Ltd,
in Australia by Random House Australia (Pty) Ltd,
20 Alfred Street, Milsons Point, Sydney, NSW 2061, Australia,
in New Zealand by Random House New Zealand Ltd,
18 Poland Road, Glenfield, Auckland 10, New Zealand
and in South Africa by Random House (Pty) Ltd,
Endulini, 5a Jubilee Road, Parktown 2193, South Africa.

Printed and bound in Great Britain by
Clays Ltd, St Ives plc.

For the original Fabulous Girls,
Muriel Farrell and Margaret Northeast

Contents

CONTENTS

Introduction

Manners will make you fabulous. Manners are sexy. The well-mannered get invited to more dinner parties and have a wider array of friends and colleagues who admire them. These are the basic tenets of *The Fabulous Girl's Guide to Decorum*.

The idea for this book came to us gradually over the course of one too many encounters with the socially inept, suffering through bad dinner parties and enduring thoughtless comments. Nearly once a week we would find ourselves on the phone or over tea, railing, 'They didn't even put food out until 11 p.m.! There was no music at all!' or 'She showed up to the cocktail party in jeans and a charity fun run T-shirt' or 'We ran into his ex and he didn't even introduce me'.

It began to add up. People are rude and inconsiderate to each other every day and in every circumstance, and what's worse, they don't seem to realize it. Perhaps they just don't know any better. In addition to being vexed by the inadequacies of others, we were crippled by an inability to correct the offenders. As every well-mannered person knows, to correct someone else's breach in etiquette is itself an infraction.

Unless, it finally struck us, we were experts.

And after a lifetime of passionate interest in the subject and experience in a great many milieux, surely we had become experts in etiquette. Having lived as single girls, party girls, married women, out-of-workniks, professionals, world travellers and fashion addicts, we knew the world and, frankly, the way it ought to work.

The essential equation of etiquette is simple: be nice and assume niceness in others – just like your mother said. Beyond this basic belief, of course, there are specific details for situations, but the foundation is always the same.

Manners are an integral part of good citizenship. Consideration for others and not only for one's own wants and needs is necessary if a person is to be a valuable member of her world. When people of varying cultures and economic brackets must, increasingly, live side by side, etiquette becomes a modern requisite. Pleasant manners are just plain more appealing than bad manners. Behaving in a thoughtful way helps both morally and aesthetically to make the world a better place.

There is a kind of woman who understands this implicitly: we've named her the Fabulous Girl. You know the Fabulous Girl, don't you? She's Holly Golightly, the girl you must have at your cocktail party. She's smart, fun, stylish and, of course, beautifully well-mannered. She's the friend who always knows when you need a shoe-shopping expedition to lift your spirits. She's the one who calls you after your disastrous dinner party and insists that she had a marvellous time. She's the girl you admire, the girl you want to be.

No-one is born perfect, and we all have a learning curve towards good manners. And so this book is both a celebration of the fully formed Fabulous Girl and a primer for the Fabulous Girl in training. The life of the modern woman is wonderfully full – work, friendship, romance and sex (we know they aren't always the same thing) are all vital to her happiness. In *The Fabulous Girl's Guide to Decorum* we will set down modern rules for every circumstance – from bedroom to boardroom – so that we're all armed with the appropriate arsenal of etiquette. Because you need to know how to handle a one-night stand just as much as you need to know how to set the table.

To illustrate this learning curve we've included the FG as fictional heroine throughout the book. Consider her as a guide to ease the journey to good manners.

Contrary to popular belief, manners will not make you a bore or a snob. Quite the opposite: individuals who possess skill with etiquette are admired and desired for it. If you are well mannered, people will want to come to your dinner parties and will want you at theirs. Manners can make you fabulous, girl – a Fabulous Girl.

The Workplace

'I was praying this morning that you wouldn't be wearing that skirt. And here you are,' sputtered Claire, a woman with a shape that women's magazines refer to euphemistically as 'pear', and my boss.

Now, I hate Monday mornings in general, but on this particular Monday, I had entirely forgotten about my job review. I was a receptionist at Corp Train, a management training firm that was as lame as it sounded.

I was silently horrified. Anyone can criticize my typing speed but never, never my style. Especially not Claire, who's idea of fashion was Annie Hall meets Laura from *Little House on the Prairie*. And to add insult to fashion injury, I was being critiqued by a person whose teeth were loaded with poppy seeds.

'We really believe in bringing people along here at Corp Train. We really do,' she continued, taking my silence as acknowledgement of sexy-skirt-guilt.

I had woken up feeling pretty good. Hair not too terrible. I wore my slightly see-through, long black skirt because it looked fabulous. As always, I wore it with completely opaque tights, so it was entirely respectable. Biking to work, I'd been thinking about how not so very bad my job was. Nobody expected me to care about the corporate training sessions the company ran. Being a receptionist did not exactly tax a girl. And as soon as I figured out what I wanted to do with my life, I'd be able to put all my energy and free time into that thing...whatever it would be.

I mean, who cares about a review for a job you don't care about? Now it was sure to be my last day. This is how it went:

'It's just not appropriate for a corporate environment. At Corp Train we have to be seen as a team, and that team is professional and impeccably groomed.'

Was she also saying my hair was messy and I needed to use deodorant?

'So Step One, buy some more modest clothes. I know that's a quick fix, especially for someone like you.'

Like me? She didn't know me. I've only worked here three months and she'd said little to me other than hello and good night.

'There are two types of people in the world.'

'Really, only two types?' I asked and gripped the arms of my chair. Claire nodded emphatically and continued.

'Type A and Type B. Type As are stars. As soon as they walk into a room, you know it. Heads turn and they command an audience. Super-confident. Then there are Type-B personalities. These people are mild and shy and are often afraid to speak up and join in group dynamics. You are a Type B. Which is fine, but it means that you're not a natural leader. There is room for both types at Corp Train, so there is a place on the team for you too. It's just not a very mobile position, if you see what I mean.'

I don't know whether it was the B or the A in me that felt it was the right moment. For two things. 'I think next Friday should be my last day. And, Claire, you've got all sorts of seeds in your teeth.'

Even though it hadn't been what I'd expected that sunny Monday and my bank balance meant that my actions should have sent me into terrible anxiety, all I really felt was relief

and a perverse sense of power. And as I've learned over
and over, nothing takes the edge off like a new pair of
shoes and a bottle of Chianti with my two best friends,
Eleanor and Missy.

In those days, Eleanor, Missy and I all despised Mondays,
the launch pad of five days of Jill Jobs, those nowhere jobs
we all begin with such as temping or waitressing. Over the
weekend it was possible to start feeling a bit fab and self-
determined. But back at a job you hate, the sheen of your
weekend self-image quickly tarnishes. We'd been best
friends since university, where we met in Intro. to
Twentieth-Century Art. We bonded over the fact that we'd
all come from small towns. Missy and El knew exactly how
I'd felt growing up, dying to bust out of rural boredom.
Although we were ambitious, stylish, smart girls, we had yet
to get it together. I wanted to write, Eleanor wanted to art
direct and Missy – well, she was just vaguely ambitious.
Eleanor was a production assistant at *Kitchens* magazine
and Missy waited tables at Dominic's, where after my Type
A stand-off I too donned apron and corkscrew.

A month later I was not feeling quite so brave about my
new life. What if Claire had been right? A Type-A person
surely would have bounced right into a better job by now.
Sure, I had started to phone editors looking for freelance
work, but it took me an entire day to build up my nerve
each time. Was I a B? Or had Claire just branded me as
one?

I had moments of wanting the drones at Corp Train to
pay for all the minor humiliations I'd endured under them
all those months. As I'd cycle through the city, dropping off
CVs at restaurants and temp agencies, I started to compose
a letter that would really blast them. I thought of sending it
to Claire's boss. I'd outline all the inefficiencies that I'd
been witness to as a receptionist. The thing about most

execs is that they're so arrogant that they think the receptionist doesn't notice that they're using the FedEx account for personal use, that they're taking hour-and-a-half lunch breaks at least three times a week or that they've been doing it in the fax room with the new trainee when the boss thinks they're working late on that big account. And in particular, I'd outline Claire's utter incompetence as the office manager. I knew for a fact that she made all her personal long-distance phone calls from work.

I thrilled to the thought of Claire being brought down to size.

And then I had what I am sure was a very grown-up moment. I just thought better of it. I was on my way to leaving those kinds of jobs behind. Who cared what a bunch of suits thought of me? And let's face it, they wouldn't have thought much of my letter anyway. Claire's boss probably hired her in the first place.

Work

For no other generation has work been so central to a woman's sense of self. Work has, for many a woman, entirely replaced the identity she may have had in previous times. The work the Fabulous Girl does – or wants to do – is critical to her. While it is still unusual, it is not unheard of for a woman to forgo motherhood and be satisfied with a life that is defined solely by her career.

For several years of her adult life, an FG may work towards her ultimate career goals without pay. She may take a less than challenging job just to pay the bills. The modern woman makes these sacrifices with long-term happiness in mind. Although it may cause her some anxiety, she is willing to give up traditional standards of security in the short run to have the life she's after in the end.

At the start of this particular career trajectory, it may be difficult for the outside world (and her family) to understand what the FG is doing or where she thinks she's going. Her life may seem a mishmash of waitressing jobs, volunteering, 'projects' (usually creative in character), courses, classes and travel. Indeed at times it will even seem to her as if it's all adding up to nothing. Somehow, by her late twenties or early thirties, an FG finds that it all has a way of coming together. All those experiences, along with her superior charm and grace, are suddenly exactly the right combination for the FG's dream job.

The Fabulous Girl acknowledges and thanks the women who have paved the way for her generation to enter the workforce. She appreciates that she now enjoys nearly endless career choices. But, an FG is not afraid to take advantage of her style and beauty and the benefits these attributes may reap for her in the course of her career. The FG notes the advantages in the workplace of being a young, confident, sexy woman. A self-assured woman carries her wit, charm and intellect with her wherever she goes. Men and women will treat her with respect because she demands it, not merely with words but with action. She knows she deserves the job, the rise, the success, the man and the flat. She's a Fabulous Girl.

Entering the Workforce

You are what you wear

One of the keys to the Fabulous Girl's success is her sense of style. Of course she is intellectually or financially brilliant – or both – but what we're talking about here is what makes the FG succeed beyond other smart women. She knows how to dress, and while she may not be rich (yet), the FG simply loves clothes. She can put together a head-turning outfit from cheap chic shops and vintage finds. She knows how to apply make-up and never leaves her home without lipstick. She is always stylish and well groomed.

The Fabulous Girl reads fashion magazines from around the globe both for pleasure and to keep up with what's going on in the world of style. She window-shops on her lunch hour and before cocktails. While she is never afraid to try new looks, she knows what suits her body type and sticks to it. Why does any of this matter? Shouldn't this be dismissed as wanton vanity? Rubbish! The Fabulous Girl understands the importance of appearances and doesn't get in a knot about whether wearing lipstick makes her a bad 'sister'.

An FG knows that great style commands respect from employers and colleagues: it reads as self-respect. Employers are impressed when a staff member makes an effort with her appearance, as it demonstrates that she cares about the work she does and that she wants to be a good representative of her company. An FG appreciates that first impressions count, especially in the workplace. Stylishness is an enviable trait, and the Fabulous Girl relishes being envied, even copied.

The way you dress can definitely influence your success at work. When your boss is trying to decide between you and the smart but sloppy woman next to you for that management promotion, guess who gets the job? Dress for the job you wish was yours. Every workplace has a subtle dress code beyond the basic rules written up in your employee's handbook. Take your cues from your boss's own sense of style (unless he or she is a slob). And please, no whining that it's not fair. Life is not fair – these are the tricks to winning the not-fair game.

WHO YOU KNOW

Nepotism is still the most unjust but effective way of landing a good job or freelance gig. Remember the film *Six Degrees of Separation*? When you are looking for work, there is something to be said for asking everyone you know, even your parents, who they know. Make sure, however, that it's a firm connection and not just someone your best friend's boyfriend met once at a barbecue last year. Those are more desperate measures. As an FG gets older, her friends will get into better positions and she will benefit all the more. The reverse is also true. A successful FG is also a confident one and therefore not afraid to help a friend develop her own career.

BRAINS: THERE FOR THE PICKING – YOURS INCLUDED

When you become successful enough, you will eventually get the call: 'Hi, my name is Felix. Fifi gave me your number. I'm dying to get into floral design, and I wondered if I could pick your brain sometime?' You will roll your eyes and look at your already packed schedule, but you should also be flattered, and you must oblige if at all possible. Everyone needs help at the start of a career – you did, didn't you? To balance universal karma, and to be polite, you must dispense whatever advice you can. How much time and mentoring you offer will depend on your schedule, of course, and on your assessment of the asker's potential. But remember: everyone deserves a chance. If you're the one requesting aid, there are very specific rules that must be followed in order to graciously maximize your brain-picking:

1. You are asking for someone's time, their most valuable commodity, so make it sound like a request, not a demand.

2. Do your homework. Aim for two or three answers, addresses or names you'd like to get out of the conversation. Don't just chat; you can't ask for a brain-pick if what you really want is a new pal.

3. Keep it brief. (See 1.)

4. Pay the bar, café or restaurant tab. The generous pickee may offer to pay, particularly if they're financially successful and you're a struggling newcomer. You must refuse (so choose to meet someplace you can afford).

5. Remember all the favours you ask for now – and start storing up lore to share when your turn comes to be asked.

APPLY YOURSELF

As a newly minted college or school leaver, the Fabulous Girl needs to find herself a job. Depending on her level of education and her field of study, she will either enter at a junior level in her chosen profession or accept a Jill Job to tide her over until she finds her niche. In either case, an FG should never sell herself short. Peruse the ads in the local and national papers and check out the trade publications for your desired field. A girl can find a multitude of entry-level jobs that may satisfy her rent cheque and lead elsewhere. An FG should certainly also apply for jobs she's not quite qualified for. For example, if she's just getting started in her freelance writing career, she should still submit her CV for that associate editor job. Even if she doesn't get an interview, she will get her name out there. Likewise, she should ask others to keep an ear open for interesting job opportunities.

An FG always updates her CV and keeps various drafts of it on her computer. She may at various times in her professional life need to adapt her CV for different jobs. For the dream job, an FG will pump up the volume of her related experiences in her coveted field. Everyone either lies or embellishes on their CV: an FG does it with style. Use different fonts for your contact information and name, embolden your headings, experiment with margins and spacing to build a strong one-sheet CV on yourself. Whatever is most exciting about your expertise should be placed first. For Jill Jobs, less is more. You do not want to appear too smart, accomplished or ambitious or an employer will sniff out that you'll be gone in six months and therefore pass you over. Dumb yourself down for these just-for-the-money jobs.

Cover letters are a must. Never fax or e-mail a CV without a cover letter. Always take the trouble to address it to a specific individual – never to 'Dear Sir or Madam' – and always state the job you're applying for and where you saw the ad; if you heard about it from a contact, state who that person is. At the close of the letter offer to submit references or samples of your work if requested. Never send scripts, showreels or audio cassettes unless invited to do so; it will only annoy the potential employer.

Some advertisements for jobs do not give out the company's name or phone number, so following up may be difficult. If you can follow up, wait one week; if you have not heard from the potential employer then call, fax or e-mail a brief note asking after the status of your application. Polite tenacity does pay off.

INTERVIEWS

The dreaded day of the interview has arrived. An FG is always impeccably groomed and chooses an appropriate ensemble for her moment of truth. Trouser or skirt suit – it does not matter which – but looking professional, even if the office is casual, is a must. When an FG arrives at the scene, she does so at least ten minutes early. This will not only ensure that she is perceived as punctual, it will also give her time to regroup. Ask the receptionist not to announce you immediately, but to direct you to the Ladies. An FG always wants a final look in the mirror to straighten her hair and the like before being introduced. She also wants to hang up her coat beforehand. The whole impression must be one of looking together and organized, not out of breath.

During the interview, be it one-on-one or with a panel of interrogators, always look your questioners right in the eyes. Keep your hands folded in your lap; never fidget. Smile as much as possible, except when offering serious answers. Have a couple of questions prepared for your interviewer. This shows that you have done your homework and that you are considering whether this is the job you want. Do not be afraid to be funny: humour is often a great tool for winning a person over. After all, who would you rather work with, the funny smart girl or the deadly serious smart girl?

Shake everyone's hand again as you leave. Follow up immediately with a note or e-mail to say thank you for the chance to meet with them. While an e-mail may suffice, a real note goes further. So break out the stationery if you really want the gig.

Again, if one week passes and you've heard nothing, a second follow-up is necessary. This may be a phone call to the person who interviewed you. You might also grill the receptionist on whether the job has been taken. If it's still open, leave a message or send an e-mail to the appropriate person. Beyond three calls, however, you become an irritation.

Jill Jobs

There will, in all likelihood, be several years when the FG will be forced to toil at a job she loathes and doesn't lead anywhere – Jill Jobs. Waitressing, temping, reception – each a classic Jill Job – all are stops on the road to future fabulousness. An FG will always perform these duties with dignity, if not pride. You may feel like an idiot serving sandwiches to bankers in a boardroom, but doubtless they are very happy you are doing it. Smile and keep your seething to yourself.

There are upsides to this kind of employment: the hours are usually fixed and can be established in advance, these jobs are universally easy and no-one expects you to care that much about them (well, OK, your boss wishes you did, but let's get real). This last point is crucial. When you walk out the door of your reception job at 5.02 p.m., you can leave it behind. The FG will not wake up in the middle of the night thinking, 'Oh, my God! I filed the Masters folder *after* the Nicholsons!' Never.

The lack of emotional involvement means that the FG can easily be engaged in some other, more meaningful endeavour. Whether she spends her evenings (or mornings, as the case may be) working on a screenplay or studying Spanish, the

FG is able to put her heart into the things she truly cares about during the Jill Job phase of her life.

Any Jill Job should be treated lightly. A Fabulous Girl always has a greater plan, and reminding herself of this can help ease the burden of her current drudgery. Do not take it seriously when you are harshly criticized for ordering the wrong type of toilet paper or coloured paper clips. These things really don't matter and every FG knows it.

When you are meeting people there is nothing wrong in leaving until last, or even omitting altogether, the details of your Jill Job. If you meet a new person at a cocktail party, you can with a clear conscience say, 'I'm working on a proposal for Channel 4' and not add, 'That is, when I'm not clearing tables at the Le Club Très Cher'. The first statement refers to who you are; the second is just about your pay cheque.

Be Nice to the 'Little People'
Minions, Gophers, Lackeys and Other Entry-Level Jobs

RECEPTIONIST

Behold the pillar of corporate culture: the receptionist. She is tomorrow's Fabulous Girl. In fact, more often than not, the receptionist is already more fabulous than all those who hover about her desk and look down at her with scribbled messages she cannot read, letters that need to be typed or packages that absolutely must be overnighted even though it's already five o'clock.

Contrary to film noir notions of gum-cracking, nail-filing, supine femmes fatales, receptionists work hard. And these smart, ambitious, educated young women control everything. They determine which of the corporate drones they babysit get calls they need or their messages delivered, whose proposals and letters are typed accurately and promptly – all of those tedious chores that make business buzz.

Belittle her and your life can be made a living hell. You must smile, remember her name and use it regularly, enquire about her state of mind or health. Offer to get her a coffee when you are getting one for yourself. Introduce her to clients when appropriate. Above all, she must be made to feel a part of the team. Remember: today's cute little thing behind the desk may be tomorrow's Fabulous Girl – and your boss.

If you find yourself in this very position, never allow an employer to raise his or her voice to you, call you names, insult you or touch you. The best course of action in these circumstances is a swift correction at the time of offence: 'Please, you do not need to yell at me' or 'Do not swear at me'. Forget such phrases as 'You hurt me when you do that'. That sort of emotional revelation is only for personal relationships. Be consistent. If you're getting nowhere with your reasonable demands for decent treatment, you may have to move on. After all, it's only a job.

COURIERS

Quite often these dishevelled boys (and increasingly girls) arrive looking like extras from *Easy Rider*. Their tough-guy demeanour intimidates many who find themselves trapped in lifts with them as they sweat and curse into their mobiles. But really they're just hard-working, hard-playing people who, in another life, work as musicians, writers and actors. It will not take too much time from your busy day to ask a bike courier how he is or simply to say hello. Remember, they risk life and limb (and often those of pedestrians and drivers) rushing about town to ensure that your diskette arrives within hours.

Personal Assistants

Akin to owning a Porsche or sporting a Rolex, hiring a personal assistant is, for many, a status symbol, not a necessity. If you happen to be the Countess of Peoria and cannot survive without a young thing at your beck and call, then at least remember to treat your PA humanely. Just because this assistant is looking after parts of your personal life (manicure appointments, picking up your dry-cleaning) does not mean that you are any less obliged to treat her professionally. It's a job like any other, and you and your PA must agree in advance to the limits of the job. Yes, she will pick your kid up after school. No, she won't wait in the car for you outside a party at 2.30 a.m. If you are asking her to go beyond the established boundaries of her job, then *ask*, don't demand. A PA is a person, not a Porsche or a Rolex, and sending her home crying will not make her respect you or work harder for you.

When you are dealing with someone else's PA, remember that she knows better than you do where you rank in her boss's hierarchy. You may think you are on a first-name basis with the countess, but be guaranteed, if her PA doesn't know you, then the countess doesn't consider you worthy of the A-list. If you want to ensure a place on the Rolodex or have your call returned, chat up the PA. Be polite, not pushy. Give a PA attitude and there is a good chance that she will snitch – and more times than not the countess will side with her.

Trainees

Like other baby steps up the career ladder, the trainee has one-toe-in-the-door status. Often unpaid, trainees do the work no-one else wants to do. They are also often very eager to please – too eager – and this can lead to abuse from those in positions of power. They tend to work in industries such as film, television, magazine publishing and advertising in which large egos mask small minds where civility is concerned. Don't stand for it!

When you are a trainee, you need to be wily to get the most out of your job. Many people don't know what to do with trainees: they need direction from you. You can be cheerful about doing crummy jobs. You can also use your cheer to guilt people into giving you something more interesting to do. Zone in on one person at the job who is likely to respond to you and give you a break: 'I'd love to stay late to wrap the cables for you tonight, Vaschlov. Do you think sometime this week I could ask you some questions about f-stops over lunch?'

If there is a trainee in your workplace, try to give her interesting tasks to do as well as the jobs you'd rather eat bees than do yourself. Remember, she's there for some experience in your field, not just to do clerical work. Most will be very happy if their jobs are a combination of drudgery and interesting work they can boast about later.

If you have benefited from the helpfulness of a trainee, don't forget it. She did not type up your contact list just for the sheer thrill of it – she's angling for future kindness. Be willing to write letters of reference or allow your name to be added to her CV.

On-the-Job Etiquette

During the months or years spent in entry-level jobs, an FG will, unfortunately, have to put up with the worst rudeness of her life. Even though most people have experienced some junior position themselves, the majority forget about it by the time they are making lots of money. The fact that there are so many uncivilized people in the workplace is a condemnation of our standards of success.

As an FG becomes more successful, she must remember not only how she was treated at the beginning of her career, but how she wants to be treated always. In cases of poor manners in the workplace, the only thing an FG can do is to stand up for herself. Point out that the offender's conduct is unbecoming. Offer a swift, strong reminder that it is unacceptable and that you expect to be treated civilly at your place of work. If the entire office is wretched, you must still deal with people individually and in the moment. 'Jo-Jo, you seem to be unhappy with what I'm presenting here. Is there something you'd like to talk about?' will shame most people into better behaviour.

If this tactic does not work, you will have to have a more direct conversation with the person who is treating you rudely. Make an appointment and get right to the point: 'Maybe you don't realize you're doing it, Jo-Jo, but I'm noticing that when I make presentations during meetings, you make it obvious that you dislike what I'm doing. I'd love to hear your comments on my project, but this is just not a productive way to go about it. Not only do I find it difficult to work this way, I think you're setting a bad example for the junior members of the office.'

No-one likes a confrontation – not even rude Jo-Jo. It's a rare person who won't back right down at this point. Of course, she will make up all sorts of garbage about having a tic in her left eye, which you will have to accept. But you will notice a marked change in her behaviour at your next board meeting.

On those rare occasions when these tactics fail, it will be necessary to treat these etiquette offenders like very small children. Every single time they snap at you or make sarcastic remarks, you must walk away, saying, 'I'm available to talk whenever you're ready to speak civilly'. Of course, this is a giant bore, but you must not accept the kind of rudeness that borders on abuse.

You can also talk to your boss about the level of office etiquette if you feel it is interfering with your work – and of course it is. This will be much harder if your boss is rude, but you must try. The Fabulous Girl must rise up and lead the revolt to a civilized workplace!

RESPECTING WORKSPACE

A person's office, cubicle or workstation is a very personal place. People adorn them with family photos, plants, cards and pictures. A desk can be a sanctuary. Remember that people require personal space even in a place of work. There are rules that must be adhered to lest you become an invader and declare a turf war on the grey carpeting.

USING SOMEONE ELSE'S DESK

People are territorial, especially in impersonal venues where they lack a sense of ownership and the freedom to relax. There is nothing that sets off a person more than walking into her office or cubicle to find Bingo from accounts using her phone or computer. If you need to use someone's equipment, ask first. Very few will say no, but all get slightly miffed if not consulted.

WHO'S LUNCHING WHO?

You may feel that the precious hour-long break at midday is yours to use as you please, and of course, strictly speaking, that's true. A savvy FG, though, will keep an eye on whom she spends her lunch time with, in order to better play the office game. There will always be people at your workplace you naturally gravitate to, but be careful not to spend every lunch with them. It's a good idea to occasionally break into other lunch cliques just to maintain a rapport with members of the office. Go ahead and sit with the guys from production even if you might be more comfortable with your best work pals. You never know how these other connections will help you. It's also a smart idea to invite colleagues, especially superiors, to share lunch even when you don't have a specific schmooze reason. But remember to take mental-health lunches, when you ditch the work gang to wander alone and remind yourself that you are an entity that exists away from business.

LUNCH HOVERING

In many workplaces, an hour's lunch break is simply out of the question. What has replaced the brown bag in the park is nuked fare at the desk. If a person has decided to forgo an absence from the office, she still requires ten or so minutes to actually eat. It is very rude to disturb people's food intake by thrusting reports in their face or asking them to come and fix your computer or put through phone calls unless they have expressly asked you to do so. Regrettably, this is very common practice in an office environment. The maximum interference you can reasonably get away with is to ask to see them after they've finished eating. Conversely, it is not impolite if you are chowing down on your ciabatta roll to tell your colleague that you would be happy to help them out when you've finished your snack.

TELEPHONE HOVERING

These are those, often in authority, who will assume that whatever it is they are doing is far more important than what you are discussing on the telephone. These people will stand over you and eavesdrop, smiling all the while, pretending to be cool with your being on the phone when in fact they are not. They are assuming (often rightly) that it's a personal call and that this means they have a right to hover. They do not. You may have to put your friend on hold and ask the hoverer to leave, or turn your back to the hoverer and hope he or she takes the hint. If you have an urgent message you need to get to someone who is on the phone, do not hover: write it down on a Post-it note and stick it in front of them. Then go back to your own space. The person will come to talk to you – after the phone call.

RETURNING PHONE CALLS AND ANSWERING E-MAIL

The most efficient and well-mannered business people return business calls by the end of the business day. Or at the very least they have their assistant do it. Of course this cannot always be the case. If you are too busy to get back to people the first day, you must do it by the next business day. This rule also applies to responding to e-mail. Do not simply ignore messages and assume that their senders will get back to you. If you do not know a caller or e-mailer then the message is of lower priority, but it still deserves your diligent attention – after all, it might be from someone you want to know.

CHATTY CATHYS OR CARLS

If you do not have your calls screened at the office and you get calls from a friend at inconvenient times – or worse, the friend just won't shut up – then you need to take polite action. As soon as you recognize the voice of your too-chatty friend, let him or her know how much time you've got: 'Hi!

I've just got a second before I have to run into a meeting. How are you?' And if that doesn't work, you will probably have to interrupt just to get a word in. Don't be afraid to lie: 'Sorry to cut you off, Bingo, but someone is at my door. I'll talk to you on the weekend, OK?'

E-MAIL ETIQUETTE

There is no denying the efficiency of firing off a note to someone without getting slowed down by the distracting small talk that can jam up phone communication. But as in every other aspect of work life, there are concessions to be made for etiquette. Not all missives can be sent by e-mail: some messages are only appropriate coming over the phone or sent by regular mail. This is especially true in the summer, when many people keep irregular hours or take holidays. It's important to know not only where to reach people, but also by which means to reach them. The main problem with e-mail is that people check it in different ways. Some are obsessive, while others only look once a week. The onus is on the message sender to be sure the e-mail gets through.

The main considerations of business e-mail etiquette:

1. It's perfectly acceptable, in fact preferable, to conduct business transactions by e-mail. Most people working in offices have their e-mail program running at all times and will receive their messages almost as soon as they're sent. Making appointments and sending memos can be done most efficiently online. Do track your e-mails or ask for an acknowledgement, though, to be sure your message has been received and duly noted.

2. Business Letters. Important correspondence, especially of a legal nature, shouldn't be sent online. E-mail is not reliable enough. What's more, the way you write a letter changes dramatically when it must be printed on paper.

Faxing or mailing forces the writer to consider her words more carefully than she would with e-mail. Those extra minutes could make all the difference between sending an overly angry letter and not.

3. Humour. Wit does not travel well across the Internet. Be cautious when making humorous observations or remarks when replying to e-mail. Tone is very difficult to gauge, and with the casualness of e-mail, people often misinterpret the written word and you end up sending three e-mails explaining your joke.

4. Spelling and Grammar. By all means, reread e-mail before you send it: bad spelling and grammar, especially when writing to a new business associate, do not speak well of you.

5. A Final Word of Caution. Remember, with any e-mail correspondence, once you click on 'send', it is out of your hands, so exercise caution with sensitive subjects, or you risk offending someone or giving the wrong impression.

CHEERLEADING

Companies or organizations need to believe that what they do is vital to society. This belief is expected to be carried on the overburdened shoulders of their staff. Now, our FG may not buy into the corporate rhetoric, but she has to appear to or risk insulting the people who pay for her monthly credit card bill. No-one is saying that you have to head up the corporate softball team, but you must keep your this-is-a-bunch-of-crap thoughts to yourself.

GOSSIP

Everyone loves it, but no-one ever thinks they are the subject of it. Gossip has its uses, such as learning of forthcoming resignations that will give you a chance at a new position. But gossip can often be backstabbing and petty. The Fabulous Girl learns to distinguish between the two; she indulges in the positive, useful kind but refrains from participating in the negative kind. If colleagues are beginning to diss someone, simply bow out saying, 'I really like so-and-so.' This usually puts a swift end to negative words. This is not a matter of being prissy but of building a reputation. Imagine that what you're gossiping about is overheard by the subject of the gossip (this happens all too frequently in offices). Can you really trust everyone in your whispering circle not to spill the nasty thing you said about Bingo's BO? If people see that you're not a gossip, they'll trust you all the more.

Promotion Etiquette

HEY, THAT'S MY JOB!

It is always a sad day when Bingo, the dolt who sits next to you, gets the groovy job you've coveted for weeks. Despite all your best efforts, you were passed over. While you may choose this as a quitting moment, you are still under Fabulous Girl obligation to be gracious. That means smiling and shaking Bingo's hand, joining in group toasts after work and giving him suggestions for office redecorating. Why bother, you ask? Because although you may really want to slam your computer across your desk and rip the phone from the wall, your boss is watching how you react. You may also need Bingo in his new position. And remember, it's not Bingo's fault he got the job you wanted.

Sorry, I'm a success!
Professional jealousy: When green isn't your colour

When you are the lucky girl and that new job and its glorious responsibilities are all yours, the standards of behaviour remain the same. If your friends are still stuck in Jill Jobs, the gap between you can intensify. First of all, tell them immediately. Do not hide your good fortune for fear of hurting them; that would be condescending. If their reaction is less than stellar, you must still be enthused and excited. This may jolt them out of their selfishness – outbursts of delight are often contagious. A small, self-deprecating joke can do much to calm rough seas. Once the announcement is made, then move on and ask them how they are progressing in their career battles. Appearing aloof because you are embarrassed by your success will only widen the gap; besides, you may be underestimating your friends.

If, however, you are the Jill Job girl and your best friend is the new executive, hide your jealousy. Of course you are jealous – everyone knows that – but to speak of it or display it in any mean behind-the-back way is unacceptable. If the successful friend is a real friend and you are frustrated by your lot, confessing your jealousy to her one to one may get you sympathy, but only if it's done in a gentle manner. Better yet, confess your feelings to a disinterested party (say, your mother). Remarks meant in jest, such as references to 'sleeping with the boss' or asking 'Who did you bribe for that job?' only show bitterness, not wit. Restraint is always the best option when dealing with such irrational emotions as jealousy. A truly Fabulous Girl is happy for her friend and can use her friend's success as inspiration for her own career. Competitiveness is not the same as jealousy.

WHEN YOUR GOOD NEWS IS ANOTHER'S BAD NEWS

Feeling gratified that you got that long overdue promotion, yet have a stabbing pang of guilt knowing that your good fortune meant another's demotion or firing? What do you say to that person? The behaviour here is simple common sense and sensitivity. Do not gloat or rant about your new position. And lend a sympathetic ear to your less fortunate colleagues. They may be bitter and not want to talk; this will depend on the nature of your relationship prior to the restructure. So let their reaction guide you. But be reasonable: they cannot expect you to not be happy or to not discuss your new work at all. Timing matters. When you learn of their misfortune, tell them you are sorry and keep it simple. They should, likewise, congratulate you for your good work. Both sides need to be gracious. As with athletes, it all comes down to good sportsmanship.

OOPS, I'M NOW YOUR BOSS!

Even though you really wanted the position, it can be slightly traumatic to become a manager for the first time. If you've always been part of a team, it's difficult to suddenly be captain. But if you're going to take the job, then you must behave like a boss. Think about the great – and the terrible – managers you've had in the past and about their style of governing. The best leaders are clear about what they want and expect from their staff. Let people know what you need them to do and don't avoid letting them know when they aren't doing their jobs correctly. Try to do this in a pleasant but firm manner. Don't apologize for telling people what to do, but don't do it with anger either.

Being witty and stylish at work often means that the Fabulous Girl becomes chummy with colleagues. This is natural and advantageous, but when you get that promotion and become the boss, feelings and expectations alter drastically. To smooth this change over, you will need to add extra honey to your already stellar vocabulary. When assigning tasks to your former equals, ask them gently: 'Would you mind terribly getting that report in tomorrow?' They may expect you to treat them differently, with either leniency or brutality, but you cannot. Nowhere is it written that to be in a senior position you have to be rude or cold. Not making an acute change in your behaviour will reassure colleagues that you're the same old, clever you, but now you just need to get them to do stuff. They'll do it because you are you.

YOU'VE BEEN A BAD, BAD GIRL

As an FG it will never come naturally to you to get cross with others. But as your career develops and you gain more responsibilities, you will have to learn how to give criticism to the people who work under you. This can be extremely stressful to a nice girl like you. But there's no getting around it, so you may as well learn to do it with some grace. The mistake that many managers (even those with experience) make is in either becoming angry with their staff when they've made mistakes or giving criticism in a way that comes off as an apology. Neither approach is useful or gracious. Remind yourself that all you're really doing is giving someone information. When letting your assistant know that you need her to be on time, remain calm and be very clear about your expectations: 'I need you to be here at 9 a.m. every morning when the phone starts ringing. Can you do that? Great.' The same should apply in more difficult situations: 'Your behaviour in that meeting was inappropriate. If you have a problem with the way your colleagues do their job, please can you frame your criticisms in a respectful manner. I don't want to have my staff calling each other names in meetings.' By remaining calm, you both express what you need to express and allow the criticized person to retain his or her dignity. People don't like being criticized, but most will respect you for being straight about it.

DON'T HATE ME BECAUSE I'M YOUNG

Many young women are taught that older women broke through all sorts of barriers to make life better for the next generation. While this may be true, don't expect a lot of help out in the real world, honey. Older women had to do much clawing to get to where they are; they had to ignore their feelings of guilt and 'niceness' to be successes. So when the Fabulous Girl enters the workplace and expects mentoring, it may be more than her elders can take and it's possible that you will get the cold shoulder. They may see you as a threat or be irritated by how much easier your lot is as a young woman today. You may have to work very hard to win these ladies' trust.

Of course there are exceptions. In these cases, the older women are themselves Fabulous and will take great pleasure in 'discovering' an emerging Fabulous Girl. As time goes by, the generation that paved the way will retire and be replaced by Generation X, a generation that can take their equality more for granted and can, therefore, be more secure with younger women.

Moving Up

COZYING UP

You're ready to make a move up, and now it's time to get tactical. The Jill Job style of leaving work behind at the end of your shift will no longer serve you. If you want more responsibility (and money), you will obviously have to start giving more. You won't have to surrender your entire life to your work, but you will have to appear more flexible about your time. Try to spend more time with the senior members in your work or field. Book appointments with your boss to present your ideas. Ask your editor out for coffee or cocktails to talk over pitches rather than just sending e-mail. Quietly advertise your achievements. This doesn't have to be creepy. Just state the facts: 'I'm so thrilled about this positive review of my book.' 'I'm really proud of this issue of the magazine and I hope you'll enjoy reading it.' 'The Big Huge Company finally agreed to sign on with us. I shook on it over lunch with the MD.' Many women feel uncomfortable bragging. Get over it. Letting people know how valuable you are may not come naturally to you, but it's key to your success. You can't gain recognition for something no-one knows you did.

SCHMOOZE OR LOSE

The art of the schmooze is a Fabulous Girl's best party trick. Networking, as it is known among serious-minded individuals, means attending a social or professional event with the hidden agenda of making business connections that will further your career. If the occasion is social, then you may want to go for a little more sex appeal in your clothes than you would at work. A cocktail dress is a must, as are heels, and a bit of red lipstick never hurt anyone. This is where flirting comes in handy – not overt sexual innuendo with your boss, but rather witty repartee with a well-timed hand on an arm for emphasis. Laughter, partnered with an insider's observation on the state of whatever topic is at hand, goes a long way to impressing future colleagues.

If you are attending a professional affair, then your dress

must be toned down; even a smart trouser suit will suffice. You may look more 'workish', but what comes out of your lips should be no different than that at a party. Professional events can be dreadfully dull, so the charming, witty, intelligent person will stand out.

And remember, people like to work with people they like. They can't like you if they haven't met you. On Monday morning, an editor will call the freelancer she had a laugh with on Saturday before she calls the person who merely pitched her project through standard means. It's not fair, but it's the truth.

SOCIALIZING: BE MEMORABLE NOT MOUSY

Socializing can make or break a Fabulous Girl's career. Shyness in the professional realm will not be tolerated: cordial and outgoing will win the world every time. In order to be successful, you must be memorable, not mousy. Be the first to extend your hand and introduce yourself; never wait for a forgetful colleague to make the introduction. If conversation lags, make a witty observation about a cultural event or, better yet, enquire into the social habits of the person with whom you are conversing. Always know the latest restaurants and boutiques in your city, see a couple of films and read at least one novel a month. Everyone will remember the young woman who told them of a great Persian restaurant or wonderful feature in *The Times* she just read and who entertained them with her charm.

PARTIES: THE LIFE-OR-DEATH EVENT

As the Fabulous Girl's career moves forward, she will have to learn to choose between social invitations. This gets simpler the more successful she becomes. Big bashes, be they web site launches or charity balls, can be missed (unless, of course, you want to go for fun). Hundreds of like-minded individuals packed into one stifling venue will ensure little opportunity for networking. You will get further sharing a single dinner with a publisher or MD than you would from a month's worth of stale carrot sticks at events. The exception is, of course, if the Fabulous Girl's company is hosting an event or is in any way involved in it. Award banquets, despite being tedious bores sometimes, are *de rigueur* for those who want to keep climbing the ladder.

Self-promotion ensures you will be noticed. Herewith is the Fabulous Girl's checklist for self-publicity:

- Get yourself on all of your professional associates' party lists.
- Attend everything (or at least as much as you can stomach).
- Make a few well-positioned friends so you can tag along to more exclusive events.
- Ask for introductions to people in positions of influence.
- Send thank-you notes to hosts and hostesses.
- Send e-mails to people who give you their cards.
- Remain in contact with people you have met who may be influential.
- Invite important people out to pick their brains.
- Get your name in the media.

Socializing with Colleagues

CELEBRATING TOO OFTEN

Certain types of industries have a multitude of professional events that all employees are required to attend. For the

KIM IZZO *and* CERI MARSH

standard Christmas party and summer barbecue, you may drag your spouse or significant other along to alleviate boredom. At these faux parties, your mate is obliged to make nice with your boss and generally act as if this is the most fun he's ever had. And you, of course, are then obligated to do the same for him at his company's faux parties. But apart from these twice-yearly occasions, your date may decline without consequence. This leaves you to determine how many bowling nights you need to attend. Sometimes blowing off steam with colleagues is beneficial – you unwind with and bond over a couple of martinis – but never be afraid to beg off for personal time with other, non-work friends.

ONE TOO MANY

When out enjoying the company of your colleagues, in particular at the office Christmas party, you must keep tabs on your alcoholic intake. Office parties are not like other parties, at which you are surrounded by friends who think your drunken imitation of a table is hilarious. Too often things occur at company get-togethers that you may want to forget but that colleagues will be reliving for months. Repeated trips to the mistletoe with Bingo from marketing will not go unnoticed, nor will falling asleep and drooling on your boss's husband's Hugo Boss. Every individual's tolerance for alchohol is different; learn what yours is and respect it, or lose respect the next day.

YOUR PAL, THE BOSS

Office Memo to All Employees: it has come to our attention that many of you have discovered that Employers Are People Too, which will explain the many friendships that have developed between the drones and their Queen.

All those hours spent together, and before you know it, you actually like the boss and, hey, she likes you too. She laughs at your jokes, you compliment her on her new shoes. If she's chummy with everyone in the office, you have little to worry about. But if you are her only or best work friend, it's like being teacher's pet – you may fall out of that vital office-gossip loop and become the subject of it instead.

Do enjoy what the boss's take is on Bingo in marketing plus other insider notes. But don't share personal information about your colleagues with your boss or drop her name to them: 'You know, Paula prefers files to be stacked like so.' Others will feel wary around you if they sense your allegiance is to the boss and not to them. Do take your friendship out of the office, particularly on special occasions like birthdays. No matter how friendly you are, don't confess your sins to your boss; skip the tales of that weekend drugs binge or your tryst with Bingo at the Christmas party.

Do be professional at all times: no slacking or missing deadlines. And don't expect preferential treatment.

HOW TO ASK JUST SOME OF YOUR COLLEAGUES TO A PARTY

With so many people working eighty hours a week, the lines between work and personal life can blur. A person's career becomes her lifestyle too. That said, devising an invitation list to a cocktail party at your place can be like walking across a minefield. Must you invite everyone you work with to your special event? What if you only want to invite one or two office mates? Of course you can be selective. Be low-key when inviting colleagues, and ask them, in turn, to be discreet.

Office Romances

TURNING DOWN GENTLY

It will often occur in the Fabulous Girl's life that a colleague will come on to her. If the man is unsuitable, the simplest and most painless way to thwart his advances is to state firmly, 'I never date anyone I work with.' This well-played move allows the rebuffed male to bow out gracefully.

If, on the other hand, one evening over one cocktail too many with an office mate, some serious kissing gets going, don't fret. Neither of you is fourteen years old. So you did a little harmless smooching, big deal. But it would be badly done on the part of the FG not to deal with it immediately. If this new relationship is not to move beyond this one time, then the FG should swing by his desk the next day, look him straight in the eye and let him know all is friendliness. Don't rely on shooting furtive glances at each other as a mode of communication. And above all, don't kiss and tell.

BIG BOSS SEX

There is one pervasive myth about the workplace that needs to be dispelled: never sleep with your boss. This is propagated by those who have never known the pleasures of such an exciting affair. Never underestimate the sexual pull of power or the ecstasy of lying on that big desk of his. The only word that must apply is *discretion*: it should remain a secret until both parties know the extent of their feelings.

At least once in our lives, we will work for an object of forbidden desire. The way he hangs on your every word, the way he tells you how brilliant you are, the way you get more nervous than usual when presenting ideas to him. Everyone else has left for the day. Then it happens. The two of you are working closely on a project. He brushes your arm. You look at him, you smile and suddenly you're stripping him of his shirt, tie and mobile phone. He stops you: 'We can't do this, you work for me, it's a small office.' You both agree it's inappropriate, but the previous months of sexual tension take over and you do it.

Now what? The risk of big boss sex is not to your career: the danger lies in what your colleagues will think. Of course you're fabulous and smart as a whip, so any promotions or special attention you garner, you deserve. But why put doubt into the minds of those you work with? You must never discuss the affair with colleagues, nor should any confessions or complaints from peers ever pass your lips when you are intimate with him. Pillow talk involving office gossip is always déclassé.

Never expect him to go easy on you at work. Avoid secret smiles and flirtatious eyebrow raising. If your affair becomes public knowledge, count yourself out of office gossip sessions: you are now the juiciest gossip going.

It's better not to say anything about your affair unless there is something to be said. Moving in together or getting engaged are times to come clean. Know that you have some difficult decisions ahead about the wisdom of remaining in your job and that if you do remain, your personal relationships with colleagues will be forever altered.

If the romance ends, you must decide if it is tolerable for you to continue under his employ. If it is, then silence is more important than ever. Failure to keep quiet can cost you your job, the respect of your colleagues and your self-respect.

We Fabulous Girls have to accept the fact that we do get more attention than others. If that attention comes from people in power, it's not always necessary to take the high road and turn away from what could be an exciting affair. Just do it with your eyes wide open: know the risks and decide for yourself.

When you're the sexy boss

Just can't stop thinking about the sexy new guy you hired last month? He may be the hottest thing to walk through your office in years, but before you ask him out for drinks after work, slow down a minute. Ask yourself honestly if he does his job well and whether you would respect him as an employee if he wasn't so fit. Then force yourself to consider all the ways this fantasy fling could come to an end. Can you picture yourself explaining this to *your* boss? Are you sure there's no way for Mr Hotstuff to be hurt by an affair with you? Do you trust him to be discreet? It's natural for people who work together to find themselves in sexually charged situations, but remember that as the more powerful person in this situation, the responsibility falls on you.

What You're Worth and When It's Not Enough

You're overworked and underpaid – so do something about it. Chances are that your employer knows that you are indeed undervalued but is counting on the Fabulous Girl trait of modesty to save money. Don't fall for it! Asking for a rise should be straightforward: 'I feel I deserve a rise' is easier to say out loud than you think. If you dispense with stalling chit-chat and smoothly state it straightaway, then the words are out there and it's your employer who must deal with them. Be ready, of course, with reasons why you deserve more dough. The worst that can happen, as the cliché goes, is that she will say no. Try to elicit the reasons for the refusal. Does your boss feel you're not worth more money just yet? Is it a budget issue? Can she agree to give you a rise in six months if you meet certain goals? Then the next course of action, including whether you'll be job-hunting, is up to you.

Bidding Adieu

Quitting is a highly underestimated skill. There are many reasons for an FG to leave a job, not the least being impending dismissal. One should always see the signs of trouble and resign. Nothing is less fabulous than being fired. However, consider first the possible economic benefits of a tidy severance package.

When it is obvious to both employer and employee that things aren't working out, invite your boss out for coffee or ask for a quiet word in her office. It is inappropriate to fuss or struggle through lengthy explanations. Simply say, 'I'm giving you my month's notice.' And bear in mind that one month is the minimum expectation; bailing out on your colleagues in less than that ensures that your reputation will be soured. Be pleasant; smile a great deal, even if you despise your employer.

Despicable colleagues, lousy pay or lousy work are all fine reasons to move on. At some point in every Fabulous Girl's life there comes a time when she looks around at her temp office job or her section of the restaurant and decides enough is enough. Try saving cash so that you're not trapped in a nowhere job when you feel the need to walk.

Contrary to popular belief, quitting a job does not grant you free rein to air your every petty grievance with your boss. Unless you are asked for specific reasons, do not give any. Your employer should accept your resignation gracefully and with slight remorse.

If you are leaving for a better job, you need to be particularly gracious. Let your boss and your current colleagues know that your new job is the kind of opportunity you really can't pass up, but don't go on and on about how great it's going to be. No matter how well you handle this scenario, you will quickly become *persona non grata*. Don't take it personally: people have to start imagining a workplace without you, so it's natural for that to start as soon as you break the news. A month may seem like no time at all to irreplaceable you, but it's not. Make your current files and contacts immediately available to the person who will take your place. And even if you're leaving a nightmare workplace, don't grouse about it at your new job.

I wasn't sure, but I think it annoyed Missy that when we were at a party, I'd tell people that I was a free-lancer and sometimes not mention the restaurant at all even though I was working as many shifts as she was. Maybe because she got me a job there when I was really desperate for cash. Maybe because she wasn't doing anything except waitressing herself.

Eleanor thought it was a sensible thing to do. But then it's Eleanor's theory that if I just went to enough of the right kind of parties I'd become a successful writer. I couldn't see the wisdom in her philosophy at the time, but because out of the three of us, Eleanor was doing the best career-, boyfriend- and flat-wise, I had to listen. It should be noted, though, that Eleanor was breaking another of her own dictums: you can have a great job, a great boyfriend and a great flat. But only two at once.

I was working on fluffy stories for the most part, tiny pieces about which cocktail urban scenesters were drinking or where to buy the best stationery. Instead of making me depressed the way the stupid work at Corp Train had made me, this kind of stupid work was making me really happy. And I was beginning to get decent assignments. I think the editor for whom I wrote about drinks and notepaper felt sorry for me. So between shifts at the restaurant, I was working on my first feature! I guess it was this story that made me stop mentioning my Jill Job when I met people.

Which is how I came to my terrible final night at Dominic's.

I was tired to begin with. Working all day, running around doing interviews and then having to show up at the restaurant for the dinner shift was taking a toll. The place was packed. And who walks in but Robin Hood.

In first year English he'd strolled into class with his thick blond hair cut into a long bob that grazed his chin. I'd whispered to Eleanor, 'Look, it's Robin Hood'. Bizarrely, his name turned out to be Robin Katz. Close enough. I pined silently for him during smoke breaks for the next three years.

Now he'd cut his hair, but he was still cute. Of course, I'd seen his name and picture in the paper over the years since school and would stop channel-hopping when I spotted him on a panel discussion. His first novel had been a big success. Awards, film deals, rumours of a New York agent. He'd been a confident guy at college but now he had the additional glow of a person who knows that he's being recognized.

And of course, because that's the kind of luck I have, he and his date sat in my section. None of the other waitresses (bitches!) would take the table for me. The date was looking around the room to see who was looking at the two of them.

I was doing my best to seem OK with the whole thing, but of course I was mortified. And he was mostly nice about it. 'That's great that you're getting into freelancing part-time,' he said. 'Do you think the kitchen would make the chicken penne without garlic and onions?'

'Well, it's not so much part-time. I mean, I'm really doing it all the time and just doing this on the side. When does your next novel come out?'

'It comes out here in the spring, the following September in the States, France and Germany. You know what my dream would be? Can I just tell you what I want and you could get the kitchen to do it for me?'

'It's not really that kind of place.'

'Oh, really? Couldn't you ask them ... you know, for a friend of yours?'

'I just don't think so.'

And then he made a weird gesture, a kind of 'I'm really sorry to hear that' shrug. And we didn't chat after that. I just brought their food and then at the end, the bill.

At the end of the night when I was cashing out my bills, my boss asked me why I hadn't told him my famous friend Robin Katz had just wanted a small change to the menu. What was my problem? Didn't I know that he wanted celebrities to feel comfortable in his restaurant? Didn't I realize this was the service industry?

Being lectured by the boss was something all the waitresses were accustomed to and usually allowed to pass through us like vapour. On this night, though, I was actually listening. 'You're right,' I said. 'And I can't serve anyone anything ever again.'

You'd think he'd have appreciated my candour. He did not. The screaming went on and on. I gathered up my things and left.

It was a cool night and riding my bike home, I imagined the damp air cleaning the restaurant off me.

Missy and Eleanor sat up with me that night, drinking red wine we took from the restaurant (and usually replaced but, to be honest, not always). I can admit now that I was feeling pretty low.

'I'm all washed up at twenty-six. That's it. I can't even make it in the service industry,' I wailed.

'Maybe you can get your job back,' said Missy. 'He never stays angry for long.'

'Don't be crazy,' said Eleanor. 'Pull yourself together!

This is all going to end up fine – you're fabulous.'

'But I have no skills,' I whimpered. 'There's no such thing as a job where you're paid for being really fun at a cocktail party!'

'At least, not without having to have sex with strangers,' joked Missy. We howled.

The girls were very nice about trying to cheer me up, but I still drank way too much and don't remember why I thought sleeping on the rug beside my futon was a good idea.

The next morning there was a message on my machine. It was my cocktails-and-stationery editor. 'Listen, there's an associate editor position opening up here. Interested? They need someone right away. Thought it might be right for you. Call me for more details.'

Well, it turns out that Eleanor was right in a way. I had absolutely no qualifications for the associate editor job at the magazine. But no-one cared a bit. The editor and the managing editor who interviewed me seemed far more interested in the bars that I went to and the places I shopped and the bands I was listening to. After I told them that I'd like to write articles about all these things, I could just tell they were going to offer me a job. And I started thinking about the clothes I was going to need.

'Sorry to interrupt you. Is there anything you need done?'

I had to bite my lip very hard to suppress the hysterical laughter rising in my throat like a swam of butterflies. Standing in front of my desk was Ben, my temporary assistant. Adorable, helpful, eager Ben. Our first two weeks together had been awkward. I couldn't get over the guilt of asking anyone to do anything for me. But I must say I was also starting to like it. It wasn't just that having Ben send faxes or call the courier company saved me time, it was also the way he looked at me. It was no secret around the office that my assistant had a little thing for me. He was really supposed to be helping out all the lifestyle editors, but he was spending more and more time at my office.

On one level I knew Ben was my employee, but on another level, he was one of the cutest boys I'd ever met. And that's probably the only defence I can reasonably make for the fact that I started sleeping with my assistant.

We were working late (and there was no expectation for him to work late). Ben was putting together a contact list for me and I was working on a story. At 9.30 he came into my office and put his head down on my desk in mock exhaustion. At first I just messed up his hair in a friendly, you're-so-funny kind of way. Then my hand was on his neck. Then we were snogging on the desk.

I guess I didn't really see what I'd done could be the source of trouble until we woke up the next morning. I opened my eyes and Ben was looking at me. Gazing is perhaps the more appropriate description. I think e. e. cummings calls these kind of eyes 'love crumbs'.

'Good morning, sweetheart,' he whispered.

I knew I was in danger of being on the business end of a schoolboy crush, not to mention lawsuit. I'm ashamed to say this didn't stop me from having some quite spectacular morning sex with him.

'Do you like him?' asked Missy.

'She likes his bum,' cackled Eleanor.

'He wants to meet you guys,' I said, which just made Eleanor laugh harder.

'Well,' offered Missy, 'if you want us to meet him, we can go to a café or something. When is his birthday? We could take him out for his first legal drink.'

'OK, OK, I'm going to break it off. His three-month

contract is about to end anyway. What if he decides to tell my boss?'

'You should have thought of that before you started pawing him,' laughed Eleanor.

Ben did not tell my boss about our little affair. In fact, he seemed entirely relieved when I suggested that the end of his contract should be the end of our tryst. Honestly, it would have been more polite of him to pretend to be slightly more crushed.

Society

I had this great new job. I could even use the 'c' word: career. And what this career girl needed was a new grown-up wardrobe. One Saturday after I'd been paid, I beamed into one of a long line of chic boutiques I normally avoided, a too-depressing-to-merely-window-shop shop. But now I had money to spend and I needed trousers. Great trousers. But as any girl knows, trying to find the perfect pair is like trying to find the perfect man: next to impossible. You try on all the styles, but they each only fit one part of you. Great around the bottom but too short in the leg. The right cut for your legs but too tight, or baggy on the bum. Or they made your thighs look like you've always feared they look. I didn't want truth, I wanted fantasy trousers.

So when I pulled on one leg of these stunning brown herringbone hipsters, I knew it was going to be a short fling, not a long-term relationship. I stepped out of the mirror-less changing room (making a mental note to never shop in a store without a mirror in the changing room again) and looked in the three-way. My bum looked OK, but it was my size 12 thighs sausage-cased into a size 10 that said 'We can't see each other any more.' The pert salesgirl smiled. 'How are they?'

This is where my buying edict comes into play: never buy anything unless it's fabulous. The trousers were close, but I knew I'd never get past seeing my second-rate self and all her insecurities every time I walked past a window or a mirror. I sighed. 'Do you have these in a size 12?' The sales-girl smirked. 'Noooo. We don't order stock in that big a size,' she meowed. 'Not unless they're small-fitting.' Which, she implied, these weren't. It was me that was big.

Horrified and humiliated, I jumped into my own clothes and bolted. Then it hit me: she was rude. What a horrible thing to say, and what a bad salesgirl! I knew that I could never be that rude to someone. Was it so difficult to make someone feel good when they were obviously feeling bad about themselves? To feel better, I went to my favourite shop – perhaps not as fancy, but they know me and are always sweet – and treated myself to some retail therapy. They were very polite to me.

As I was walking to the station loaded down with splitting shopping bags, all I could think of was getting home, cutting the tags off my new clothes and hanging them up. Then a much-deserved nap and a bubble bath.

It was during this reverie that I heard my name being called, and sure enough, there was Missy waving at me from across the street. My heart sank – she would want to talk for hours. That meant coffee, no nap and no bubble bath. A dozen excuses flashed before me as Missy ducked traffic to come to my side. 'Hey,' she said, 'haven't seen you in a while. You haven't called me back.'

There it was, best-friend guilt. The trouble was that I had been crazy busy, and Missy is not someone you can talk to briefly. And she didn't have e-mail. Missy didn't even own a computer. There was no real reason for ill feeling between us, but I felt uncomfortable about how well things were going for me while she was still waitressing at Dominic's. This imaginary rift was why I hadn't called her. And now she was raising it.

'I'm sorry, I've been swamped. I don't want to call for just five minutes, and I never seem to have time for longer.'

Missy smiled. She always forgave me. 'Want to grab a bite and catch up?'

I gulped, put on my best liar face and fibbed, 'Sorry, honey, I can't. I have to rush home and work on a piece that's late. Next weekend, I promise!'

Missy looked at me, I thought, suspiciously. Could she see right through my self-absorbed self? 'OK, next weekend, for sure, right?'

We hugged goodbye and I walked away, feeling terrible. Then I passed a homeless person sitting on the ground not even asking for a handout. The twine handles of the bags were cutting into my palms. Weighed down with wardrobe and guilt, I took out a couple of quid and put it gently in the man's hand. He smiled and said, 'Bless you'. I smiled back. It has always been my secret fear that I would end up alone and a bag lady. And that if I don't treat the people who care about me better, maybe I will.

Society

Beyond the workplace, a whole world awaits to be conquered with grace. The Fabulous Girl is a good citizen of her neighbourhood, city and country. Prizing elegance, beauty and good taste, her major contribution is an aesthetic one, but the FG is also the epitome of democratic social interaction, able to converse with and befriend a politician and a plumber equally. She is a truly social being, recognizing that her demeanour and behaviour will affect those around her (and being as dynamic as she is, there will always be many around her). She not only respects but celebrates certain rules of etiquette, setting an example that, if followed by her fellow citizens, would make for a happy and harmonious society.

Quite naturally, then, entrance into society is an important phase for the Fabulous Girl. It involves the careful and wise selection of a new group of people who are different from the company she kept at school and university.

This does not mean that an FG necessarily wants to 'trade up' on all her social contacts, but she should start making conscious decisions about how and with whom she wants to spend her time. She needs to think about how she conducts herself and, yes, what that looks like to the rest of the world. The more gracefully she can handle life, the more she will attract like-minded, gracious people.

Your People

Although an FG's appearance – in fact, her whole life – may seem effortless, it's not quite so. It takes a team of professionals to make her life run smoothly. As you get older, you need to take the task of developing your People quite seriously. The best way to build your list of contacts is to consult with other FGs. When you're at a dinner party and notice that the table looks especially beautiful, remember to call the next day (to say thank you, of course) and ask if the hostess wouldn't mind telling you which florist she uses. Occasionally people are secretive about these things, but for the most part they will be flattered that you noticed their good taste.

The People you may need at one time or another are:

- Hairdresser
- Beautician
- Masseuse
- Cleaner
- Dog walker and/or cat sitter
- Florist
- Shrink
- Accountant
- Doctor
- Dentist
- Lawyer
- Caterer
- Personal trainer
- Tailor
- Cobbler
- Mechanic
- Dry-cleaner
- Travel agent
- Nanny

TIPS FOR YOUR PEOPLE

If your hairdresser is also the owner of the salon, it is not necessary to tip them anything. But you should leave a tip with the person who washed your hair. A pound will suffice, more if you're feeling generous. If, however, your stylist does not own the salon then a 10 per cent tip is more than adequate. You can either give the money to the receptionist, or direct to the stylist.

You may want to tip your manicurist, facialist or waxist, but don't feel you have to.

The Fabulous Girl Aesthetic

MAKE-UP

The Fabulous Girl should buy at least two new lipsticks per year, a spring/summer shade and an autumn/winter hue. Signing up for make-up demonstrations at your local department store is an inexpensive way to learn proper technique and to try out a cosmetic line before you shell out. Always err on the side of less-is-more for daytime. Nighttime, feel free to put on some more eyeliner and a darker shade of lipstick. An FG needn't be made up 24/7, but she will always prefer to face the world confident that she doesn't look like something the cat dragged in. In other words, the FG will consult her mirror before taking leave of her home.

HAIR

Hair should always be sleek and clean. Get a haircut every three months. Length will be dictated by trends, your face shape and, most importantly, your mood. Short hair feels liberating and looks exactly right on many faces. But, longer hair can create a glamorous look that men, friends and colleagues will appreciate. And without a doubt, long hair is better for sex.

Hair is difficult, so don't be afraid to bring in the professionals. If you've got a big day for which you want to look polished, book an early morning blow-dry. A gala night? Stop by the salon on your way to have your stylist put it up for you. After all, a girl can't be good at everything.

GROOMING

An FG isn't confused about what it means to look after her looks. She knows she can shave her legs and still be a feminist. Of course during college everyone experiences some ambivalence in this area, but once you're twenty-four it becomes tedious.

Unless you are a woman of leisure you probably don't have the time – or the money – for the whole shebang (a full-on spa day for a facial, massage, manicure, pedicure, wax, etc.) every week. But everyone should do the whole shebang at least once.

Do-it-yourself spa treatments are relaxing and sensual. An FG should consider setting aside an hour or two for Saturday afternoon sorcery at home to make herself feel (and look) good! In the summer, get a bikini wax a couple of times so you're not worried about anything escaping from your swimsuit.

WARDROBE MAINTENANCE

If you are spending money on fab clothes and shoes, look after them properly. Ask other FGs about the best dry cleaners, cobblers and tailors in town. Once you've found places you like and trust, use them often so they get to know you and look after your investments well.

KIM IZZO *and* CERI MARSH

FLAGRANT FRAGRANCE

Perfume is for up-close, intimate encounters, not the entire marketing team at Monday's breakfast meeting. This rule makes no distinction between Avon and Chanel. It is not only bad manners to force others to smell you across the hall, it is in poor taste and shows that you don't know how to wear it properly. Here is the correct method of fragrance 'dressing': if it's eau-de-cologne, spray it into the air and walk into the fallout; never spray it directly onto your clothes or skin. If it's *parfum*, then a dab behind the ears and in your décolletage is all anyone ever needs for daytime. If there is a consistent fragrance felon in your midst, it is not inappropriate to take her aside. How do you know if you're wearing too much perfume? Ask a friend to embrace you then to take a step away. If she can smell your scent only when you are hugging, then you're fine. Otherwise, it's too much. Perfume addicts, be thoughtful: we love to see and talk to you – we just don't want to smell you.

Nice and Rude

RUDE TO THE RUDE PERSON

In etiquette there is an important rule: don't be rude to the rude person. And we know this can be excessively challenging. When someone queue jumps, makes some disgusting sound or gives you attitude, all you want to do is retaliate. In the most conservative reading of this rule, though, you must not. You certainly may stand up for yourself and let the rude person know that you, in fact, are next in line. You may also let people know that they have hurt your feelings with their behaviour, but you must try to express this in civil terms. Tell your boyfriend that you'd appreciate a phone call when he's going to be a half-hour late for dinner rather than simply locking the door.

When confronted with a breach in etiquette, simply remark upon it: 'Wow! You are being so rude. How do you do that?'

On the flip side, if you see someone making an etiquette mistake that is not rude but merely incorrect, never point it out (unless the person is a child or someone very close to you). If your dinner guest picks up the wrong fork to eat his salad, it is very badly done to point out his mistake. In fact, some hostesses would actually make the same mistake themselves to put the offender at ease – well played.

PUNCTUALITY

It might seem bizarre to need to say anything at all about punctuality, but alas, the need exists. The only reasonable excuse for lateness is, well, a reasonable excuse. Traffic was much worse than expected. Your kids both threw tantrums as you were trying to get out the door. You broke your leg. Amazingly, though, there are people who feel no need to give excuses at all when they arrive fifteen or twenty minutes late for an appointment.

The chronically tardy tend to let themselves off the hook by saying they've never been able to be on time. Perhaps they think this character flaw is charming. It is not. Not only is it rude to be late, but also a subtle act of control to consistently keep people waiting for you.

To train your tardy friends against this bad habit, you'll need to be fairly tough. Decide how long you are willing to wait for a friend or business acquaintance before you know you'll get irritated. Always leave the agreed-upon meeting place exactly at this point. When the latecomer calls to find out what happened, simply say, 'Oh, I assumed you'd forgotten'. People usually change their ways after hearing this a couple of times. You may get the reputation for being a strict friend, but at least you won't be kept waiting.

JUST LETTING YOU KNOW

The FG is always compassionate – even to perfect strangers. She does not let a bit of embarrassment stop her from acting in a kind manner. If the woman walking a step ahead of her on the pavement has a big wodge of toilet paper trailing from her shoe, an FG does not hesitate to let her know. Save a stranger from potentially humiliating moments arising from spinach teeth, labels sticking out from clothing, huge runs in tights or a dusty bum from having sat on a bench outdoors – as discreetly as possible, of course. This rule applies to the opposite sex too: just tell the poor guy his fly is unzipped. He'll appreciate it.

PLEASE DON'T DO THAT

No matter how much a girl loves her friends and family, there does come a time when they do really irritating things. One such modern annoyance is the passing on of junk e-mail. This might be a joke, a chain letter or a conspiracy theory. Often when forwarding these, the sender doesn't even bother to add a personal note, which is really the most impolite thing about it. If you are constantly getting such junk e-mail, particularly from certain individuals, you should send out your own multiple e-mail with a simple message: 'Please don't forward me any impersonal messages, including jokes and especially chain letters. I don't read them anyway so it is a waste of your time. Thanks.' Here the words 'please' and 'thanks' fulfil the needs of decorum (even though you're clearly pissed off).

ONLY JOKING

Other slights that some people can't seem to stop making are constant belittling reminders of your past mistakes, like that lemon car you bought online or your bad history with men, or they constantly make fun of your name. After all, they're only kidding, right? Wrong. This kind of person is passive-aggressive and should be avoided. This behaviour was only marginally acceptable at school. Take adult offenders aside and tell them to stop it, that it really annoys and hurts you and that it's disrespectful. If they don't stop, stop talking to them until they grow up.

'NICING'

Living in the urban setting provides many pleasures – variety in restaurants, access to a good Brazilian wax, cocktail parties. But so many humans sharing such limited space can also create tensions. Most of us are presented daily with the stress, temper and bad behaviour of humankind. It is more than a little tempting to correct these breaches in others, or at the very least to snap back. You know deep down, however, that neither response is acceptable.

Try our entirely successful alternative: 'nicing'. Forget *nice*'s usual adjectival purpose and begin to use it as a verb – as in 'the waitress was getting tetchy with me so I niced her'. It is the assertive deployment of sweetness that we're talking about here. This does not make you a pushover. On the contrary, nicing is a tidy piece of manipulation that can crack even the toughest nut. When the waitress becomes increasingly tetchy, you become increasingly sweet and polite, loading on the 'thank-yous' and the 'I really appreciate thats' until she submits to your will. Pre-emptive nicing is also effective in dealing with customs at your local airport: 'Good morning, here's my passport, I'm off for two weeks of sun. You must get awfully tired after the long hours you put in here. Do you guys ever get to go away?' Trust us, it works.

Funerals

Death is one of the certainties in life. Every FG will have to attend funerals. While there never seems to be a right thing to say, the most simple phrase, 'I'm so sorry', lets the grieving family know you recognize their suffering but does not engage them in a conversation too painful for them at this moment. Avoid details about their loved one's death and refrain from 'At least she didn't suffer'. Don't offer to come by and help clean out the cupboards or ask about the will. Let the family guide you. If they want to talk they will. If they respond to your initial sympathy with a nod or 'thank you', let them move on to other guests. Do not try to distract them by asking about their work or retelling a story about your latest European excursion. That is belittling even if you mean well. Call a few days later to check up on them.

Introductions, Salutations and Social Intercourse

HELLO, I'M FABULOUS

Everyone knows that introducing strangers to each other is the right thing to do, but so many people fail to heed this simple life lesson. Not so the Fabulous Girl. Here is the FG's guide to elegant introductions: as the introducer, present the junior person to the senior person. For example, 'Doctor Smith, allow me to introduce to you Bingo Jones, Bingo, Doctor Smith.'

If the status between individuals is more equal, the lady's name should be given first. If they're social equals of the same sex, any order will do. All FGs take note that the very proper etiquette is 'to you' and not 'let me introduce you to' – a subtle yet important difference.

When you are being introduced, the appropriate gesture is, of course, the handshake (no hand-kissing unless you are a deposed Hungarian prince). This is followed by 'How do you do?' or 'Nice to meet you' or simply 'Hello' – never 'How's it going?' Always make clear eye contact.

Can't recall if you've been introduced to someone before? Even the smoothest social operators run aground on occasion. A warm 'hello' covers you. If the other party says you've met before, don't argue. If you have met but you forget someone's name, just admit it. If yours is the forgotten name, laugh it off and offer your name again. And if you have the bad fortune of accompanying an ill-mannered lout who does not make introductions, don't fume, just introduce yourself. Let the lout look bad, not you. It's also much better to err on the side of repeated introductions than to assume that people know each other.

After names have been exchanged, rather than beating a quick retreat, introducers should present a brief bio of each person. This establishes some commonality or contrast, which can lead to conversation. Note: this bio should not be a crass description of someone's professional value. Thus, say, 'Doctor Smith, Bingo also collects antiques', not, 'Doctor, Bingo is chairman of Sotheby's', followed by a wink.

THE KISS OF HELLO

When the FG meets one of her closer acquaintances, it is quite acceptable to kiss in greeting. Every FG can recall nose-bashing, ear-licking, air-kissing social greetings. Such blunders may be avoided if these simple rules are followed: start by kissing the right cheek. Briskly glide backward and move in for the left-cheek kiss. Two kisses, not three (once on the cheek is very American). And, unless you're from Moscow, certainly not four. However, if you are in the line of multiple-kissing fire, go limp rather than second-guess his or her intentions. You are presumably greeting someone you're fond of, so it's lips to skin; air-kissing appears squeamish and is insulting. The kiss may result in FG lipstick prints, but a simple wipe with a finger will remove them, or you can inform the recipient about them.

PUBLIC GREETINGS

Once made, an introduction cannot be disregarded. The newly introduced cannot escape the acquaintance at future meetings. Only a very ill-mannered person will greet a familiar face with a vacant stare. Therefore, no matter how hurried you are, or even if you do not like the person, you must offer a gracious acknowledgement. If you don't want to chat, a simple wave and a blasé but cordial 'How are you?' will do. If you are in public, you may keep moving while you do this, even admit to being in a hurry. If, however, a brief chat is in order, then walk alongside the person and take your leave at a convenient corner. Never assume that you're the only one who's in a hurry. If you do choose to pause, keep it brief; after salutations, suggest calling to catch up later. Likewise, if on your stroll you spot someone enjoying a quiet moment, don't assume she's looking for company but don't ignore her either.

CONVERSATION

Language is a tool, and the Fabulous Girl must learn to use it. Of course the FG moves through life with an uncanny ability to converse with and charm others from all walks of life, be they neurosurgeons or gardeners. That's right: an FG is skilled at making anyone feel comfortable and worthy.

THE ART OF CONVERSATION

It should be simple: you talk for a bit, then I talk for a bit, I ask you a question and wait for a reply, I show some interest in that reply, then you reciprocate with some curiosity of your own. Perhaps you're familiar with it, this thing called conversation?

Recent experience would, sadly, suggest otherwise. Instead, what passes for conversation in many sophisticated circles is more like a competition for air time: I sit through your noises until you need to inhale, then I jump in and make noise until you cut me off and make some more of your own noises. All this 'me' and 'why me' just doesn't cut it in polite company. Thus we would like to present a remedial course in conversation for those in need.

1. Listen. Don't just wait for your conversational partner to stop talking. By all means add your thoughts to whatever it is they're saying. It's all too clear when people aren't listening, though. Joe is telling a group at a cocktail party about his trip to surf school in Hawaii and Jessica jumps in and says, 'Oh that reminds me of the time I lived in Spain for a summer.' If this is your conversational tactic, you can be sure everyone is thinking, huh?

2. Be aware of who you are talking to. Does everyone in the conversational circle know about Islamic banking? You don't have to avoid your favourite topic if the entire group is not up to speed on it, but you do have to be sure to fill them in. Of course, if you find yourself in the middle of a topic you don't know anything about, it's your job to pipe up and ask questions rather than sit there and get irritated. Likewise,

beware of shop talk in mixed company. Sticking for long stretches of time to conversational topics that necessarily exclude some people at a party is simply rude.

3. Ask questions. Nothing is more tedious than people whose idea of conversation is to outline their latest accomplishments. There's nothing wrong with filling people in on what you've been up to or sharing a piece of good news, but be sure to take a real interest in the other person as well.

4. Of course, in gatherings such as a dinner party, it may occur that two of your guests engage in a heated debate. As a hostess you are not to discourage this, as intelligent discussion is nothing if not entertaining. If it becomes clear, however, that the conversation is excluding all others or is going on for a lengthy period, then you should interject with a 'Sally, do tell us about your trip to Nepal...'

5. If you are the shy, silent type, chances are you tremble in fear during such social settings. But shyness is not an excuse. Make an effort by asking people about themselves, and you may develop the reputation of being an excellent listener. Of course, you also run the risk of never getting a word in, but you can't have it both ways. If you are conversing with a shy person, at least make one or two attempts at conversation. But if the person still won't say boo, it's time to move on.

EXPLETIVES

When embarking on a passionate account of your run-in with the dominatrix who stood between you and your favourite Manolo Blahniks, try to keep the expletives to a minimum. No matter how cathartic '!@%&' or '@#%$&' can be, there are far more clever ways to emphasize your point. So in lieu of Howard Stern-style trash talk, challenge yourself to think how Jane Austen or Oscar Wilde would fashion their attack. And remember, your audience is the person you're talking to, not everyone within a five-mile radius.

There are, however, occasions when swearing is absolutely acceptable or, at the very least, appropriate. If, for example, you submit a story idea to a TV producer and she rejects it but blatantly steals your idea, then referring to her as 'that fucker' helps to ease the pain. Use such language with discretion, though – among close friends and colleagues, not during business meetings or social gatherings. Even if you think your use of 'motherfucker' is hilarious, others may not.

Visits

It's always best to set a time to see friends, dates or family. If you are suddenly struck with the desire to see someone, just call first. Always assume that others are as busy as you are. If you stop by without calling, you must be prepared to find that your pal is on her way out, in the middle of something or just plain not in the mood for company.

Freelancers or anyone who works at home will, with good reason, be touchy about this. When home and work are linked, it can be difficult to make the world respect your schedule. A good friend, of course, doesn't assume that a freelancer's schedule is any more flexible than a nine-to-fiver's.

Street Etiquette

For urbanites, nothing signals the real change of seasons like street life. The moment we can burst out of our wardrobe to reveal sun-starved skin, we long to stroll, to linger, to sip lattes alfresco. There are, however, certain rules. An FG never rides her bicycle or wears rollerblades on the pavement. (A true FG refrains from wearing the inherently annoying blades to begin with.) The only people allowed on wheels are the under-two set and the disabled: everyone else must yield for buggies and wheelchairs.

As for walking along the pavement, try to avoid moving more than two (or at most three) abreast. Be aware that while you saunter at your leisurely pace, there may be a pedestrian backlog behind you. Let others pass so that they do not have to walk into the road; it is the lowest in manners to force someone into the path of a moving vehicle rather than inconveniencing yourself.

OPENING DOORS

Remember, an FG is confident in her status as an equal to men in all facets of life. However, she does enjoy old-fashioned gestures of gallantry. Allow a man to hold a door open for you. It is not degrading; it is polite. There will be many times that an FG will be able to return the favour, because chivalry is not just for male–female pairs. If two women approach a door, the one who arrives first should open it, except in the case of age or infirmity.

The two types of doors are the standard hinged door and the revolving door, and there are different rules for each.

The hinged door

Holding a door open always means pulling it toward you. If you're in a door jam in which someone else is on the other side, the door-opening obligation falls to the person who can pull rather than push – otherwise you might knock the other person over. More often than not (especially with a two-way door), men should make the gallant gesture. If you are opening a door that pushes rather than pulls, then push it open, step outside and hold it ajar for the person following. If you are just barging through alone, make sure that you do not let go of the door so that the person behind you gets a facefull. Unless your outfit consists of epaulettes and a jaunty cap, you are not required to stand there interminably while tourist groups move through your space.

The revolving door

The etiquette challenge presented by the revolving door, with its extra weight and particular design, is that the customary rules are reversed. For the rock-solid traditionalists among us, gentlemen should initiate rotation so as to make the round trip easier for the lady. A final note of caution: doubling up is forbidden, no matter how much fun it may appear. Similarly, it is not funny to trap a stranger with you in the door; if a man does this to you, remind him that it is rude, not flirtatious.

PUBLIC TRANSPORTATION

Yes, it is true, the elderly, the disabled and pregnant women *do* need to sit down on tubes, buses and trains. It is up to the FG to demonstrate to the public at large what good manners are and to offer her seat should such a person need it. It will make you feel good too.

Taxis

They can be expensive, but they are a more pleasant means of arriving at an event. However, as a Fabulous Girl, you should be aware of your options when entering a cab, especially with a date. Naturally, most men automatically open the door for their dates. This is good. However, the attire of the FG should dictate who gets into the cab first. If you are wearing trousers, then you can easily enter first and scoot across the back seat to make room for him to follow. But if you are wearing a skirt of any length, then scooting can get awkward, even scandalous – you might flash the cabbie. Anticipating this dilemma, the gent should allow his date to enter, shut the door and go around to the driver's side. Of course if it is rush hour, the FG takes command, insisting that he scoot across first rather than risk his death in traffic and force her to attend the event dateless.

Once safely ensconced in the back seat, the only remaining issue concerns driver consideration. While back seats do make excellent venues for post-party canoodling, extremes like exposed flesh or loud squealing suggest that you consider the cabbie a non-person. Just say 'Shhh.'

CARS

Asking to borrow a friend's automobile, no matter how much of a scrap-metal heap you think it is, is not polite. If there is a dire emergency, then make such a request only of your nearest and dearest: relatives first, then best friends. But don't feel thwarted if they turn you down flat; it is unlikely that you will be insured to drive someone else's vehicle. This type of risk on an infrequent driver is too much to ask of most people.

Manners for non-car owners

Most big-city dwellers can, thankfully, go through life without owning an automobile. Some, however, will choose the high cost of a car over the high stress of public transport. Since the well-heeled and the well-wheeled inevitably mix socially, these relationships can lead to a unique strain of road rage. For the vehicle owner, navigating the road of friendship with the carless can drive her around the bend. If you think your driving friend hasn't noticed how many times she's invited to go grocery shopping with you, you're wrong. If you're asking the driver for a favour, then do so; don't pretend that a Saturday afternoon foray to IKEA is a big treat for her.

Here are the keys to keeping you in the passenger seat: always offer to share the petrol if it's a long journey. On shorter trips, try to pay or share the cost for parking; it may still work out to be less than public transport. Don't assume that because your buddy has a vehicle that she wants to cruise you around the clubs every weekend. Why not offer the use of your driveway overnight and split a cab? Your friend with the car is not a bus, so volunteering her to pick up the members of your party all across town and expecting her to drive everyone home later is to make a very inconsiderate assumption. If your car friend really wants to be a designated driver, then have mercy; inebriated passengers are sure to become backseat drivers. Don't complain that she's driving too slowly or that it's silly to stop at a red light at 3 a.m. If all this seems unreasonable, you can always take the bus.

Road rage

Unfortunately the intense crowding that has emerged in our cities in the past decade shows no sign of abating. Nor does the resulting glut of ill-tempered, short-fused, poorly trained drivers on the road. Unless one is an ambulance driver en route to an emergency, then one should have no cause to drive rudely and impatiently, so endangering others.

Signals

The simplest of all good driving manners is somehow the most difficult one to convince people to respect. It's easy to use your indicator. Do this while you are moving towards your turn or before changing lanes, *not* as an afterthought while you cut someone up.

Remember, too, that if you see someone signalling, then slow down and as a courtesy, let them in front of you. It really will not keep you from making that all-important appointment. If someone lets you in, always give a quick thank-you wave to let the other driver know you appreciate it.

Horns

Yes, these annoying eruptions from cars do have a purpose. It is to alert other vehicles or people that they are getting too close to you or to make others aware that you are there (e.g. when you notice a car backing out of its driveway, you may want to alert its driver that you're there). But honking at pedestrians who are crossing too slowly or extended blasting at rude drivers only makes you the rude person.

Speed

Use the left lane if you are going the speed limit or under, not the right. If a car is coming up behind you, then move over and let it pass.

Driving too close

There's a simple rule: don't do it. Ever. It is both rude and extremely dangerous. If you are the victim, then just ignore it or slow down to the speed limit; they will then pass.

PEDESTRIANS

Please be aware that even though you are on foot, you must obey traffic signals too. People who cross before the light has changed or during a flashing green are abominably rude. Traffic lights must be adhered to for everyone's safety.

CYCLISTS

For some reason many people who choose a bicycle as their means of transportation seem to think that they are beyond the laws of the road. A bicycle is a vehicle too, and traffic lights and road signs are for cyclists as well as motorists. Know the signals for right and left. The driver or pedestrian may assume you actually know the law and expect you to stop, so when you don't and you get hit by a car or mow down a mother and child, then you are to blame. If you want car drivers to respect you, then you have to respect them. The Fabulous Girl cyclist understands all this and is able to navigate her city's streets safely and fashionably (there is nothing more chic than a summer dress on a bike).

Drivers should do an over-the-shoulder check for oncoming cyclists before flinging their car doors open.

The Well-Mannered Traveller

Travelling, whether for business or for pleasure, can be a stressful experience. But there are a few rules of decorum that can lessen the load.

AEROPLANE ETIQUETTE

Although airlines attempt to board passengers in an order that prevents traffic jams in the aisles, inevitably a back-up occurs. Be aware of this, and when you're in the middle of the aisle casually removing your coat or rummaging through your bag for gum, look behind you! If there is a queue, step into the seat section and let others pass you.

There is nothing more irritating than arriving at your seat to find all the overhead baggage compartments chock full of someone else's stuff. Follow the rules: bring on one bag, not three. Ensure that the people in the seats next to you have ample room for their belongings, and be cautious when stacking your belongings not to squash theirs. The flight attendants should ensure that these rules are followed, but most do not unless you complain – and since attendants hate complaints, they may side with the guilty party.

While most seats do recline to allow for snoozing, ensure that your chair is placed in the upright position during the meal. It is the height of traveller rudeness to force fellow passengers to eat with their food on their laps.

Keep children in their seats. Do not allow your bundles of joy to kick or poke at passengers beside or in front of them. Think this is obvious? How many times have you seen squalling brats careening down the aisles while their parents snooze? Or had your hair pulled by these angels during the flight?

When exiting the plane, wait your turn; do not leap to your feet and push ahead of others. You'll all be allowed off. If someone is having difficulty getting his or her luggage down, help them. The extra minutes will not ruin your life.

MONEY

When you've arrived at your destination and need to get a taxi to your hotel, it is wise to stop by an airport shop and buy something small. Why? Because when you exchanged your money for the currency of the country you're visiting, the chances are that all the bills you were given were big ones. You'll need small bills immediately to tip the cabbie and the porter at the hotel.

Understand the local currency. Memorize the exchange rate to ensure that the tips you give are adequate. And find out from your travel agent or hotel concierge what the tipping procedure is. It does vary from country to country, and you don't want to pay too much or too little.

LANGUAGE

A month before your journey, take the time to learn a few words and phrases in the language of the country you're visiting. A must in every language are the words for 'please', 'thank you', 'I'm sorry', 'exit', 'entrance', 'bar', 'I would like...', 'How do I get to...', and 'Do you have this in a size...'

RESPECT

Every country is unique in its customs and municipal methods. This is why you travel, right? To visit somewhere different. So you must not spend your time whining loudly to locals about how much better it is back home, or complaining about the prices, the food or the bed. This just makes you a poor ambassador for your own country.

ASSOCIATING WITH OTHER TOURISTS

Every individual varies on this. Some travellers prefer to sample local colour in every way, shape and form, and that means avoiding other Brits. Then there are long-term travellers who seek out their countrymen for a taste of home and for familiar accents. Don't be offended if your offers of an all-Brit drinking night are refused. Likewise, if you don't want to associate with people just because they're from the same country, you must turn them down politely. Simply because you bump into other compatriots on your travels does not mean you must invite them along with you.

Hotels

What follows are the general rules for four- and five-star hotels. Adjust your behaviour according to the level of service and stars of your hotel. If you're not in a five-star hotel you can tip less money.

Concierge

There are no hard and fast rules of etiquette for tipping a concierge. Some concierges have been tipped rice crackers, a simple thank-you note or even a £10 note for a dinner reservation at a fashionable restaurant. Use your judgement here. How often you use the concierge and what task he is performing should be your guide. It is fine to tip £5 for theatre tickets for a night out. If you will be staying at a hotel for several days and asking a lot of your concierge, you may want to wait until the end of your stay and tip him as you are checking out.

Chambermaid

In the deluxe hotels, you'll find chambermaids. How much you tip should depend upon how much work was required. In other words, how messy were you? Are you a total rock star slob or a neat diva? Tip accordingly at the end of your stay, and try to give it to the chambermaid to avoid confusion. £10 is more than adequate for a few nights in a smart hotel.

Porters

The proper tip for the porter is £1 per bag.

Hotel valet

Parking space is at a premium in cities in the UK, so it wouldn't be unusual to tip up to £5 for this service.

Shopping

As a Fabulous Girl ages, her taste in make-up and wardrobe need to reflect her deepening wisdom. There is much to be said for growing old graciously. Micro-minis are rarely for the over-thirty crowd.

It is a sad fact of life that people treat you according to how you present yourself. Shop assistants will treat you better if you dress the part. Leave the gym wear, comfortable as it may be, in the locker room. And as for that man in your life – yes, he will need your opinion on what to buy – get him to look the part as well. Nothing is sadder than a grown man trying on jackets in his trainers and shorts. He should wear a buttoned-up, collared shirt, because this is the only thing that will make a jacket look right. Proper shoes are also necessary for accurate trouser judgements.

Do not feel compelled to patronize only the large department stores or chains. In every urban centre, there will be local designers or boutiques that will carry unique fashions. It is wise to get to know your shopping neighbourhood and to let the shopkeepers get to know you. Get yourself on mailing and events lists to keep up to date on what merchandise they bring in. It is not unheard of for an FG to have shop owners call her when they feel that a new arrival will be just her thing.

To cultivate such relationships, the FG must be friendly and open when meeting shop owners and staff. Of course in the world of designer emporiums, there is also the Fabulous Salesgirl. She may be someone with an ambition in the fashion industry or she may be just saving up for college. Either way, the Fabulous Salesgirl treats all her shoppers – with big wallets or small – with respect. She only offers her opinions when solicited, and she only praises the choices of her clients once they have been made. She knows when you need to think a purchase over and gives you space and time rather than rushing back to you after thirty seconds to see if those capris fit.

Some salesgirls can, however, be annoying. The over-thirty

FG will naturally resent a twenty-one-year-old telling her how fab she'd look in fun-fur neon-pink hot pants. It's also irritating when a salesperson (who is probably on commission) tries to intimidate you into buying something you know very well doesn't suit you. It is therefore best, if no-one of your age or taste group is present, to ask politely to be left alone in the changing room. If there is a mirror (and quite frankly, there should be) in the room, then you needn't come out at all. If at all possible, the FG should be accompanied by a groovy FG friend.

While in the changing room, try to keep it neat. You do not have to rehang everything; that is part of the salesgirl's job, and really, who can ever refold things the way *they* want them? But bring your choices out of the changing room, or ask the salesgirl whether she would prefer you to leave them there or to bring them out.

SALES

No matter how civilized a person is, shopping is one activity – especially during a sale – that is sure to invoke Jekyll-and-Hyde behaviour. People who are otherwise gracious will jab and shove their way through racks and bins to get that 75 per cent-off cashmere bikini. Their driving motivation is not the article so much as the thrill of the deal. Suddenly, greed is good. But don't despair: all one needs is good shopping manners.

1. When searching through racks or bins of clothes, do not snatch items out of someone else's hands. Wait until the garment has been put down, or ask if you can have it. Try not to make it too obvious that you are stalking someone, waiting for her to put down the item you covet. It will only make her want it all the more.

2. Try on your clothes as swiftly as possible, in consideration of those waiting.

3. Scope out the changing room to see if it's appropriate to bring your mate in with you. He or she should either wait at a safe distance outside of the area or be in the cubicle with you.

4. Try to let others have a turn at the three-way mirror, or at the very least, do one turn right and left, then move over slightly so that another girl can see herself too. Don't be a mirror hog.

5. For extra points: a camaraderie can occur in these situations. Make eye contact and smile at your co-changers. Let people know when they look truly spectacular.

THE GENEROUS SHOPPER

A trickier manoeuvre is to let a stranger know that the salesgirl is full of it and that she does not actually look positively radiant in that lime-green jumpsuit. If you find yourself in a changing area with a woman who is being overwhelmed by a lying salesperson, you can intervene. A brief remark is usually enough to snap people out of their shopping reverie. While the salesperson is out picking up accessories for her snappy number, speak up: 'You know, that lime green is really fun, but I thought the black skirt was a lot more flattering'. This may feel like a bold move, but most women will take it in the sisterly way in which it is intended and be happy they were not parted from their hard-earned cash for something they would have regretted later.

The Fabulous Girl is a confident shopper and knows her own look well. She is secure enough to be able to share her shopping haunts with others. Imitation *is* the highest form of flattery, and it is therefore perfectly acceptable to ask an FG where she got her new leather coat and to go ahead and get one too. (This is especially true if you do not socialize too much together.) Even so, one phone call will ensure that you're not planning to wear the same outfit. If you are unsure how your copycat look will make your fellow FG feel, ask; she will undoubtedly say that it will not slight her in the least.

An exception to sharing a fashion trend occurs when an FG friend or acquaintance craves a particular garment that is one of a kind. If she is pining for a designer dress at a specific boutique to wear to the wedding you are both attending, it would be highly unacceptable for you to buy that dress. Never do this.

The Telephone

The telephone presents many etiquette issues, such as how late or how early to call someone at home. If the person you are calling is not a close friend or relative, you would be wise not to call on weekdays after 9 p.m. or before 10 a.m. unless you are expressly asked to do so. On weekends stay off the line prior to 11 a.m.

MOBILE PHONES

While it's true that there is still something inherently annoying about mobile phones (I've just *got* to be in touch at all times), they have become a regular and intractable feature of modern living. So, if you're going to be a mobile phone user – and honestly, who isn't by now? – just do it politely, please.

Mobile dos:

1. Do make your conversations brief. It doesn't matter how good your mobile is: it's always hard to hear what someone is saying on a mobile, and it's not pleasant for anyone. And didn't you say when you got your phone that you would use it just to let people know when you were running late?

2. Do use it as a dating device. If you give out your mobile

number, your pursuer never knows where you are and you therefore seem very elusive and glamorous.

3. Do use them for chatting if you are trapped somewhere extremely boring, like when there's a queue to check in at the airport.

Mobile don'ts:

1. Don't use that hands-free device – it makes you look like you're talking to yourself.

2. Don't give out your number to someone you don't want using it. This may seem obvious, but it's been known to happen that people have given out their number and then been annoyed to receive a call which cost them, if they're abroad.

3. Don't use them in restaurants, cinemas, bookshops or anywhere public (unless the call is extremely brief and you excuse yourself).

4. Don't raise your voice. Unreliable technology means that some people feel the need to scream. Please don't. No-one else wants to hear about your merger.

5. Don't use your phone while on a date. We've seen it happen.

Restaurants

TIPPING TO ENSURE PROMPTNESS

When you are considering going out for an evening, never forget to factor tipping into your budget. It is very badly played to cover only your bill and not leave something for the FG who served you. If you feel you can't afford it, stay at home. And please, save the story about how you don't believe you should have to subsidize her wage. Whatever. Just cough it up.

In a restaurant, consider 12.5 per cent to be a standard tip.

If your server was exceptionally sweet or helpful in landing you the table you wanted or in getting you out the door in time for the movie, then leave something extra. Yes, it's a lot of money, but going out is a luxury and a tip is just part of the cost.

If you're just out for a coffee, you might want to leave 50p rather than leaving your coppers.

If you've received both a terrible meal and terrible service, you are, of course, not obliged to leave anything at all. Try, though, to distinguish what is the waiter's fault and what is the fault of a slow kitchen or understaffing. If you are unhappy with the establishment, take it up with the owner or manager.

SEATING AND TABLE MANNERS

When being seated, the first person in your party should move around to the farthest seat at the table. Ask everyone in the party to give their opinion on the bottle of wine, unless you are the known wine expert; even so, ask if someone else wants to select for a change. Try to ensure that everyone is ready to order together. Then make sure that all menus are closed to signal to the staff that you are ready to order.

The FG knows that she cannot begin her meal until everyone has been served. However, it gets irritating when one person in a party of six orders a starter salad, causing lingering starvation for the other five. An FG would cancel her salad if this were the case, but if she is one of the remaining five then she will either order a starter herself and encourage others to do so, or split an appetizer, or order bread and olives – anything but glare at the poor, thoughtless lone salad eater. There is little to be done when, in a more casual environment, plates are removed as each person finishes his or her meal. But it's more often the case in these establishments that plates are left fermenting half-eaten for unappealing lengths of time. You can ask servers to remove offending left-overs as soon as the last diner has finished. In finer establishments, the staff will not remove finished plates one at a time; they will politely wait for the entire table to be done.

When the bill comes, it is time to ante up. It is commonly understood that individuals pay for themselves unless all was equally split. That is to say, if all present ordered approximately the same priced food and shared a bottle of wine, then it is reasonable to ask to split the bill evenly. If, however, the designated driver had only water, then she should not feel the need to fork out for the wine and the after-dinner Scotch. Every FG will have in her circle of friends the 'round down' bill payers. These people will consume £26.94 worth of the bill but will toss in £25, which never covers the tip. Then the rest of the party has to make it up. Do not be afraid to announce that the party is still 'short', although often these culprits will still sit silently.

UNACCEPTABLE BEHAVIOUR IN A BISTRO

An essential tenet of etiquette – don't be rude to the rude person – must be broken here. Traditionally, a well-mannered person does all she can to avoid highlighting the shortcomings of others. This jerk, though, must be stopped. Nothing says more about a person than the way he treats waiting staff. (OK, your shoes say a lot about you, too, but that's another issue.) You don't want to make his wife uncomfortable about her poor choice in husbands, so try at first to keep it light. Smile when you say, 'Whoa, you're courting waitress retaliation, there, Bob. When I waited tables, the snapping fingers thing would have made me sit on a table's orders for a good half an hour.' You must, of course,

end the night with a whopping tip to make up for the error
of his ways.

Pregnant Women

Should you encounter a mum-to-be with Chardonnay and
cigarette in hand, don't assume that she's an alcoholic chain-
smoker. It may be the first indulgence she's enjoyed in six
months. She does not need to hear from the Moral Majority.
And restrain yourself from touching her belly without asking.
It is not a puppy.

The Haves and Have-Nots: Children

Forget income – the most contentious division between
haves and have-nots in the urban setting concerns children.
The fork in the road usually starts appearing at around
twenty-five years of age and only grows more pronounced as
people get into their thirties. The child-free may think their
friendships will be unchanged by a pal's little delivery, but
they'll soon find they are wrong. Parents, necessarily, become
a little deafer, a little less irritated by chaos. Perhaps it's a
function of sleep deprivation. How can you handle the nerve-
fraying screams of your friends' bratty kids?

Carefully. If you find yourself in a restaurant with your
friends and their offspring, you may delicately let them know
that you find it worrying the way little Freddy is tearing
around the room. Of course, it's really a parent's job to
realize when her kid's behaviour is spoiling dinner for a
room full of people, but so often it goes unnoticed. 'It's just
that I'm worried about his safety. I mean, if a bowl of
steaming soup lands on his head, it could really hurt him'

is a gentle way of reprimanding spaced-out parents.

If dinner's at your place and you're afraid for your furniture and your pet's safety, it's perfectly acceptable to invite those from the kid cult over for dinner *sans enfants*. 'If you're able to find a sitter, we'd love to have you over on Saturday' is a polite way of asking people to spend an adults-only evening.

The only time you must grin and bear grimy mitts pawing your new leather trousers and conversations that can't get beyond the starting point because of child-created interruptions is when you are in the home of the children themselves. Console yourself with the knowledge that on their own turf the little monsters may actually seem quite sweet. Heck, if you're lucky, you may even get to do bedtime story duty.

Famous Friends

A strange thing happens to some people when they meet any kind of celebrity. Not so surprisingly, they want to impress the celeb. Surprisingly, though, the way many decide to tackle this challenge is to treat the celeb rudely. The dummy thinks, 'Everyone sucks up to Mr Bigshot Author. I will stand out in the crowd by being sceptical of his talent. He will be so impressed by my insightful, yet tough, analysis of his last book that he will want to be my friend.' And so dumb-dumb says to the author, 'Yeah, I read your last book. Pretty interesting. I had a couple of problems with it, but it was pretty interesting.' Celebs are usually famous for something they have done or created (with the obvious exception of royalty) and just like you, they don't like their work to be criticized by someone they don't even know. There is no such thing as being too pleasant to someone you are just meeting, and that includes celebs.

The flip side to this reaction to celebrity is well known. Almost as bad as intentional coolness towards your new celeb acquaintance is overt fawning. There's nothing wrong with letting these people know you admire them and enjoy whatever it is they do. You can even do it several times. But if you think you're going to be spending time with this person for whatever reason, you must get over your awe or you'll never be friends. Neither of you will be comfortable with your relationship.

Events

HOW TO BEHAVE AT A BOOK LAUNCH, FILM PREMIERE OR ART OPENING

The first sign of a new season is the sudden pile-up on the cultural calendar. If you have friends – or friends of friends – who write, act, paint, sing, organize charity benefits or anything else of a showy nature, you're apt to end up at a gallery opening, book launch, premiere party, fashion show or local theatre event. And you must know how to attend it with panache.

This is one time that 'fashionably late' will not do. These parties are usually quite short events that depend on a critical mass of people jamming the joint all at once.

Dress up. Think of yourself as a living set piece – if a TV camera happens by, you want the host to talk about the 'beautiful crowd', don't you?

When you have your one-on-one audience with the exalted artiste, this is not – repeat *not* – your opportunity to turn armchair critic and divulge your opinion on abstract brushwork or character development. Limit your comments to brief one-sentence compliments: 'It was wonderful' or 'I can't wait to read it'. If you don't like the work, lie. At least congratulate her on the accomplishment. If worst comes to worst, distract her by complimenting her clothes – or leave early, free bar or no free bar.

Conversely, don't sulk if your successful friend doesn't devote the evening to you. He or she is working. Another no-no is asking an author to sign your book at a later date when she has more time to pen your personal note. Get in line with everyone else. Finally, never try to be the chic insider by asking the artist how many copies of her last book sold or how much her last film made. This is like asking an accountant his yearly income.

AWARD SHOW ETIQUETTE

It's Oscar time again, or perhaps just the National Marketing Development Awards, and you've been nominated. It may be your fifth time down the red carpet or your first – it doesn't matter. What does count is how you behave. Most people attend these yearly business events because they have to, either because they need to schmooze or because they might actually win. If you do win an award, be gracious when you accept, and please be brief. Enjoy the applause, thank the right people and move on. Don't try to be Billy Crystal. If you lose then be a good loser. Applaud, congratulate the winner and enjoy the free bar. There is always next year. If, however, you are not one of the nominees and are attending for other reasons, you still need to focus on the proceedings. Never get up to leave during an acceptance speech. If you need to dash to the bathroom or to answer a call, wait for the moments in-between announcements and make your escape during the applause.

CONCERT-GOING

You must arrive on time to concert and theatre events, lest you become the annoying person who makes an entire auditorium row stand up during the opening act of *Figaro*. Likewise, unless you're about to faint, remain in your seat until the interval or until the performance is over. When an event or concert is finished, wait patiently for the rows to exit. Do not leap over others in a hurry.

If it is an outdoor event, try to keep a watchful eye on other concert-goers. If, for example, you feel you must stand up to see better, check with the people behind you and ask them if you are blocking their view. If you are, then sit down. This is especially true if it is raining and you have an umbrella. Ensure that you are not ruining the event for others.

MOVIE MANNERS

During a trip to the cinema, remember that it is a public space. So chew your snack quietly, and keep the crackling of the bag to a minimum. There are so many commercials and trailers before the main feature these days that there is no excuse to be eating at all during the film.

When arriving at the cinema, delegate the task of buying snacks to one or two in your party before you get your seats. Do not all sit down then decide you all really want nachos and get up again, thus disturbing the other patrons in your row more than once.

Saving seats for more than two people is rude. During opening weekends some people have been known to send in two friends to take over a row of seats for their posse. This is unacceptable. If you want a seat, arrive early.

Never, ever talk during a movie. Never, ever explain the

plot to your date during the movie. Never, ever translate it into another language during the movie. Never, ever exclaim, 'He's got a gun' or 'This is when she dies' during the movie.

At the end of the film, leave your seats quietly and quickly. Never just stand up and mull over the film with your date. People do like to read the credits; if you're standing you're blocking their view.

APPROPRIATE APPLAUSE

While many an FG would like to think applause is for her, there will be occasions in which she will be the one clapping. In general, applause is a gesture of approval and praise that we bestow on performers, orators and during certain significant life moments such as graduation. But is clapping always appropriate? Here is the Fabulous Girl's guide to audience manners:

1. Classical Recitals, Operas and Ballet. During such highbrow fare, it is actually inappropriate to applaud until the end of an act or concerto. In other words, you shouldn't be smacking your hands together and whistling through your teeth after every cello solo. Tempting though it may be, it is poor form to send up thunderous applause after Yo-Yo Ma's rendering of a Boccherini concerto unless the entire performance is *rifinito*.

2. Jazz. The nature of jazz allows for greater freedom of expression from performers and audience alike. It's not uncommon to be tapping feet during a night at the local jazz joint, so go ahead and clap away – after all, smoke, Scotch and applause go so well together after a roaring trumpet solo.

3. Graduations. Gentle applause is *de rigueur*. But do not stand and jump up and down as if you were at a football game. Graduations are a sombre occasion.

4. Funerals and Weddings. As a general rule, applause is

inappropriate: a eulogy is not a performance. This can also be said for weddings. Though it is quite common for the guests to clap after the bride and groom kiss, it is not proper decorum in houses of worship. However, at less formal weddings (say, in a garden), clapping can be done without remonstrance.

5. Standing Ovations. After any great speech or perform-ance, gentle applause is appropriate, and to really show your appreciation it is quite acceptable to give a standing ovation. However, it is wise to reserve the standing O for those per-formances that you felt were stellar rather than leaping to your feet in hypocritical tandem with the mob even if you despised the performance. This way the standing O remains a judgement call and retains its cultural currency.

6. Award Ceremonies. Like graduations, these events are often professional in nature, and that fact should guide your behaviour. Listen politely for the speaker or winner to finish, and clap gently, unless it's a lifetime achievement award, in which case a standing ovation may be more appropriate.

7. Applause as Frustration. Clapping can also be used to illustrate impatience when you're waiting for an event such as a rock concert to start. To this end, it must be done in unison; stomping the feet in tandem also is effective. This is perhaps not an elegant thing to do, but it is a far more civil method of expressing displeasure than other, unsavoury tactics, such as shouting or storming out of the theatre.

People in your Neighbourhood

GAYS AND LESBIANS

The Fabulous Girl moves in many social circles, and it will naturally happen during her lifetime that some of her closest friends will be homosexual. There are certain rules of etiquette in gay and lesbian communities that an FG should be aware of.

Terminology

If you are straight and are socializing or working with a homosexual person, then the correct terminology is *gay* or *lesbian*. Only if you are very close friends and only during social occasions can you safely refer to them as a *dyke* or a *fag*. Even then, you must know if your friends refer to themselves as such before you use the words yourself.

Coming out

When an FG decides it's time to announce she's a lesbian, she should share the great news with the key people in her life first. Allow for a reaction period, and in the case of parents, let them spread the news to members of the extended family. This makes them part of the process.

When an FG receives the news that her best FG buddy is now a lesbian, her appropriate response is 'That's wonderful' or 'That's great. I'm so happy for you'. Never ever remark 'I always knew it' or 'I'm not surprised'. The person in question will be hurt by such comments.

If you are friends with a homosexual person, never assume that he or she is out to everyone. When you are moving in various circles with your friends, ask them if they are out before you mention to Bingo in accounting that So-and-so is gay. This rule applies to mutual gay friends. It is the height of rudeness to out someone who does not wish to be outed.

Likewise, if you have a friend who you suspect is struggling with her sexuality, do not try to push her into admitting she's gay. While this should not be a taboo topic, you must be subtle if you think she even wants your help. If you are discussing the woes of dating, for example, matter-of-factly say,

KIM IZZO *and* CERI MARSH

'Have you ever thought of dating someone of the same sex for a change?' Let her reaction guide you.

Lastly, never assume that someone you don't know well is straight. Avoid joking with a woman about that cute guy in the xeroxing room or trying to commiserate with her about men.

AA FRIENDS

Many people have suffered through traumatic times during their lives. An FG understands human frailty. Thus if in her circle of friends there are recovered alcoholics or drug addicts, she must know how best to treat them in social settings.

If you are invited to a recovered alcoholic's dinner party, do not bring alcohol. Instead offer a bottle of fancy mineral water to your hosts. While many people involved in AA-type programmes talk openly about it, others may prefer privacy. Let the host guide you in this way. You may be curious about AA or want to illustrate how 'OK with it' you are, but you may just offend people if you ask personal questions. Likewise, don't assume that everyone but you is in AA just because no-one is drinking.

Feel free to include recovered alcoholics in your parties. It would be wise to inform these guests that alcohol will be present, but the choice is theirs. You do not have to omit libations from your soiree.

HOMELESS PEOPLE

One of the best qualities of the Fabulous Girl is her ability to transcend social gaps. She knows that if a person is on the street that it's not necessarily due to laziness or drug addictions. She understands that circumstances change and society allows certain souls to fall between the cracks. Thus, when passing a street urchin, she has two choices: give over some change or move on. Whatever her choice is, she looks the person in the eye and smiles as she says yes or no. Of course there are people on the street who are intimidating or mentally ill. In those cases it may be best to move forward without eye contact. But if poor people are selling a legitimate product such as a charity newspaper, the sale of which is specifically designed to get them back on their feet, there is no reason to run away. They are people who are trying to get by.

SMOKERS AND TOKERS

Smokers of legal cigarettes have become increasingly marginalized in our society. Yet they do exist, and the majority of them are women. There are, of course, obvious rules of etiquette for smokers, such as never smoke in another person's home without permission and don't light up at a table unless everyone has finished eating. But there are some other less obvious handy hints:

1. When going out with non-smoking friends, buy your cigarettes before you hook up with them. Don't drag the entire party to the local convenience store for your packet. You knew you were attending a party or going out; you should have bought them earlier in the day.

2. Always have matches or a lighter on hand for yourself and others. Men in particular should always carry a light: there is nothing sexier than lighting an FG's cig.

3. Offer other people a cigarette (or even a drag). You may assume you're the only one who smokes, but others may want a quick fix. Remember, you've also bummed plenty from strangers.

4. If you're a 'social smoker' at a party, bring your own

packet. Borrowing more than three cigarettes during an evening means you need your own. And make sure those three are from different people.

During social events, there will be, along with the smokers, those who indulge in drugs, be it marijuana, E or cocaine. Never pressure others to partake. This sounds obvious but many adults who are high resort to a fifteen-year-old's behaviour on this point. If you're in a relationship in which one of you tokes and the other doesn't, make ground rules. Otherwise the high person can become intolerably incoherent or pick a fight with the non-high mate.

Non-smokers and non-tokers should also refrain from criticizing those who do partake. When walking out of your office building in January, do not glare at or quip to the freezing smokers on the pavement or those huddled in the door frame. They are allowed to be there. It's the law. There is nothing less gracious than judgemental bores.

The Nouveau Riche

The Fabulous Girl may herself one day be blessed with riches beyond her dreams, whether it's her dot-com business savvy or that great promotion at the bank that gets her there. Either way, she knows how to handle her new lifestyle.

Never flaunt it. The oldest and most sophisticated families have captured our imagination because they appear so elegant. They do this by not talking about how much that new Jaguar or that weekend trip to Prague cost. That's right. If you are suddenly rich, keep it to yourself, except for family and close friends. The people who were there for you before you made it are the ones who will still love you if you lost it again. Don't turn your back on them or snub them for new, and improved, rich friends. Instead, treat people to things without being gauche. A girls' spa weekend is fun: a new Ferrari is too much. For parents or siblings, however, buying large gifts is acceptable.

Learn to tell a business acquaintance from a real friend. New money means new opportunities for others to lure you into new ventures. Be cautious.

Philanthropy is a fabulous way to use your new financial status. Research various charities that you're interested in, and then donate accordingly.

While flaunting is off-limits, an FG can indulge in gloating to evil ex-boyfriends who dumped her because they 'disapproved' of her lifestyle, or to an old nemesis who enjoyed it when she failed or struggled. It is acceptable to mention to them how busy you are because of that forthcoming trip to Paris – after all, you've only just returned from Rio.

One final note of caution for the newly minted Fabulous Girl: never name-drop. It's not becoming to anyone from any walk of life.

The following weekend was the National
Magazine Award party. Neither my nor Eleanor's magazine
were up for many awards, but we were looking forward to
the party anyway since it was a well-known schmooze fest.
This made it very much a work event. I only emphasize that
point because Eleanor was insisting on bringing Bad Ol'
Bingo along. He was her boyfriend of two (or was it three?
It was so on and off) years – one of those guys you know
for a fact isn't good enough for your best friend, but you
tolerate him for her.

Of course because I had a car and was going to drive,
figuring I wouldn't drink at a work function, Eleanor asked
me to pick her up, and while I was at it, could I swing by
and collect Bingo? Now I am a great driver – it's a particular
point of pride, and I like driving – but sometimes being the
only friend with a car made me feel, well, used. Neither of
them was ready when we agreed I'd be there, so time ticked
away and my nerves were fraying like last year's pashmina.
Even though he'd already made us late, Bingo did what
cigarette smokers always do: 'Can we stop by a store so I
can pick up some smokes?' Eleanor chimed in: 'Oh yeah,
and I need to go to a cash machine.'

This is what I hate: people think that because you own a
car, you are a taxi. When you know you're going to a party,
why can't you think of money and fags ahead of time?

Smokers are addicted; can't they just get addicted to being stocked up instead of imposing on me? Trusty old friend that I am, I drove them to a supermarket that had both cigarettes and a hole in the wall and waited and waited. Finally they got into the car and we were off.

At the party, trying to be Miss Dignified, I realized I was being Miss Dull. Horrifying. Eleanor and Bingo were off canoodling in a corner, and there I was, left to fend for myself. Despite my new job and my new wardrobe, I still had my old shyness. I hated networking and had been trying for years to convince myself that I didn't need to do it. Yet there I was among the key players in the publishing realm, people I should meet, and all I could do was smile meekly and sip a mineral water. I needed Scotch.

Then I saw her: the Obnoxious Schmoozer, laughing and flirting, so over the top that I wanted to sneer. But no-one else was snickering; they were enjoying her company. Ugh. Then she was in the midst of an intense-looking dialogue with the editor-in-chief of my magazine! I'd been trying to impress him for weeks. And there she was, charm popping out of her Versace dress.

Something had to be done. I gave myself a mental pep talk: I was brighter than she was (well, probably, I didn't really know her); I'd read her stuff, and mine was as good, if not better. And I already worked at the magazine. So why was I standing alone, too shy to chat up my own boss? That did it – I went to the bar and shot back a single malt. Then another. I was ready. I waltzed up to them and stood at their side, clutching a third drink and waiting for my chance to impress. Suddenly I could feel a pair of gorgeous blue eyes on me. It was a guy I'd never seen before, and he was staring and smiling at me from the next conversational circle. I smiled back and looked away. He was the Groovy

Guy – I couldn't figure out what a filmmaker was doing at a magazine function, but then I didn't know much about magazine functions, so I didn't worry about it. But it wasn't just his occupation that made him stand out from the crowd. He was tall and lean, and cool in his black suit. I tried to refocus on my boss only to realize that the Obnoxious Schmoozer wasn't giving any ground (how rude!). I sighed and smiled at my boss, who hadn't noticed me there in the first place. Deflated, I ordered another Scotch. It would be a taxi home tonight.

Later, I gathered Eleanor and Bingo and dragged them to the door, took one last sip of my drink and – 'Oh shit!' – Bingo bumped into me and sent it flying out of my hand and onto the trousers – honestly, right onto the crotch – of Groovy Guy. He looked pissed off, but at Bingo not me. 'I'm so sorry,' I gasped. 'Don't worry, it's not your fault,' said G.G., trying to wipe at the stain with his handkerchief.

Bingo pretended not to notice what he'd done. He was drunk, and when he drank he was a fool – a groping fool, I might add. Groovy Guy retreated back into the party and Bingo pinched my bum as he helped me into my faux-fur coat. As I wobbled to the cab, I realized that I really needed to change my socializing style. I needed to become fabulous. Not like the Obnoxious Schmoozer, but like Audrey Hepburn in that call-girl movie, *Breakfast at Tiffany's*. I could do that. And I would.

Friendship

Cardboard. No, not cardboard. Another C.
Carpet. Wet, nasty fusty carpet. In my mouth. Awful.

The phone rang beside my bed. Eleanor. 'Breakfast?'

'Or you could come over here and shoot me dead.'

'Is Missy going to come?'

'I'll call you back in a minute.'

I speed-dialled Missy. She picked up sounding way too perky. 'I'm not working after all. So I reorganized my wardrobe. By colour.'

'I'm impressed, Missy. Brunch, then, with El?'

'Is she coming alone?'

'I can't ask her that. Believe me, I'd rather not see Bingo ever again. Anyway. Shall I say in an hour at the Spoon?'

There was nothing really wrong with Bingo as a person (when sober, that is). He was smart and funny and didn't talk too much about his job at the Johnny Teen show any more. It was as a boyfriend that Bingo failed so utterly. And as I mentioned, we just couldn't have that. The last time he'd dumped Eleanor I'd made the mistake of saying I thought she was better without him. Of course, she wanted to hear that at the time, but a week later when they got back together, it was a bit awkward and I could tell that Bingo knew about what I'd said.

'Nice to see you, Bingo,' I said an hour later, settling into the booth. 'How's the show?'

'Great.'

'Tell them about your new job. He got a promotion,' said Eleanor. She beamed at him.

'It's nothing. I'm just the associate producer now. No big deal.'

'That's great. Congratulations,' said Missy, smiling politely.

'Well, it's not like he wasn't already doing more than the actual producer anyway. They're finally recognizing his work,' said Eleanor, patting his shoulder. Bingo pushed his shoulders back as if to sit up straight, but the movement also pushed Eleanor off him. She folded her hands in her lap. 'Well, we should order.'

I was dying to talk over my run-in with Groovy Guy the night before but was silenced by Bingo's presence. This is exactly why Saturday brunch is only for girls. You cannot possibly talk about men when there's one at the table. It's not that Eleanor's relationship made her uninterested in analysing the situations that Missy and I still got into, but none of us could get used to Bingo being there.

'How was the party last night?' asked Missy.

'It was great,' said Eleanor, smiling up at Bingo.

'I was bored out of my head,' said Bingo, looking around the crowded café for our waitress. 'Is anyone working here or what?'

'There's only one waitress on for this whole room. She's doing her best,' said Missy, a frown creasing her face.

'I thought it was fun. Why, didn't you have fun?' Eleanor frowned. 'Did you have a good time?'

'Well,' I said, 'kind of. I'm not really very good at that schmooze thing yet, and I didn't know very many people. Do you know that groovy guy that we spilled the drink on?'

'Him?' said Bingo, still twisting his neck around. 'Total

bastard. Finally. Bring me a coffee and the special with scrambled, bacon and toast.'

I thought Missy was going to become violent. We were going to have to leave at least 20 per cent to make her feel better about this.

Breakfast arrived.

'That was quick,' Missy smiled at the waitress.

'For a restaurant, maybe, but for a café ... isn't the whole idea supposed to be that it's fast and easy? I don't want to give you a hard time, but we've been here for forty-five minutes.' Bingo smiled as if to a naughty child. And of course, there would be no free refills for us now.

'Is that why you didn't have a good time, because you don't like that groovy guy?' Eleanor asked.

'No, I was just bored,' said Bingo. 'Print people are so arrogant. Let them do some real work for once. Like they're creating art or something. They take no interest in TV at all.'

'That's not quite true. I think they're very impressed by TV people. Probably a lot of those people would like to be working in TV,' said Eleanor.

'Why is the groovy guy a bastard?' I asked.

'He's just a typical independent-film director. Thinks he's better than anyone working in TV. The guy had his first film shown at the Sundance Festival and conveniently forgets to mention that he ever worked on TV. I know that guy from when we both worked at a cable station.'

'I know people like that,' said Missy. Even before I knew exactly what she was talking about, I felt a small fist form in my stomach. I put my fork through a chunk of cantaloupe.

'Sorry? You know people like what, Missy?' I asked.

'People who don't like to admit that they've had certain jobs.' She was smiling into her omelette. Eleanor had been working as an assistant to the art director for about five years, so that pretty much ruled her out of the discussion.

She was too preoccupied with Bingo's dissatisfaction with breakfast and film people to be really listening anyway.

'Um. Missy, do you want to explain what you're talking about?' I was trying to laugh.

'I just mean that whenever you tell people what you do, it's like you've been a journalist your whole life or something. I mean, it's great,' she told her eggs.

'And the problem with that is...? I'm supposed to meet people and say, "I'm an associate editor at a magazine, but you also need to know that I was a mere waitress just six short months ago"?'

'Oh, *mere* is it?' This time Missy was talking directly to me.

'OK, Missy, you know that I'm kidding.' I looked to Eleanor for help, but she was looking off in the middle distance while Bingo started fumbling around for his wallet.

'I've got to run. I've got a lot of stuff to do today. I'm totally out of cash. Can you cover me?' he said as he stood up.

'Of course,' said Eleanor, smiling weakly. 'Do you want to meet later?'

'I'll call you.' When he kissed her on the cheek, she looked more like she'd been slapped.

'I should go too,' said Missy. 'I've got some mere waitressing to do later and I need to do my laundry.'

'Missy. Come on. What's the problem?'

'Nothing. I'll see you all later.'

'I'll call you later, OK?'

'Whatever.'

She put on her vintage Persian-lamb coat and left. But not before putting down twice what she owed.

'Can you believe that?' I asked Eleanor. She shook her head and asked, 'Did you think Bingo seemed OK?' I shrugged.

Friendship

Friends are vital to the happiness of the Fabulous Girl. Friends of all ages, sexes and locales will enrich an FG's life by giving her expert opinions on her wardrobe, love life, career, health and all that fulfils her. Forget diamonds; society is a girl's best friend.

The Fabulous Girl is blessed with a plethora of friends and acquaintances. People naturally gravitate to her because she is charming, witty, well presented, polite, gracious, warm and an intent listener. Who wouldn't be seduced by such a presence? Since no-one is immune to the FG spell (while this may be cultivated, it is neither artificial nor a 'trick'), she will be presented with certain friendship situations that she must navigate carefully so as not to tarnish her image and, just as importantly, her self-image.

Being a good friend is not as easy as one may think: it requires effort and patience. An FG has plenty of both. Maintaining her friendships is also something that she takes seriously.

The Fabulous Girl is a girlie girl. She likes the company of women, she trusts her friends and she does not become catty at the sight of another FG.

Loyalty is indicative of her style of friendship. If you hear negative gossip about one of your close friends, put up your well-manicured fists and tell the offending naysayer how wonderful your friend is. If they still won't stop, you may be forced to walk away from the conversation.

Girl Time

How much time should be reserved for girl time? If you are a busy career woman and are in a relationship, then it may be realistic for you to see friends only once or twice a week. Those occasions may be lunch dates or cocktails in the 5 to 7 p.m. range so that you can go home for quiet time. And if you are burning the candle at both ends, you should not feel obliged to see the same friend every week. Leaving phone messages or e-mail to check in on a friend will keep you connected when you can't get together.

Try to spread your social time around so that you see a variety of people. Your friends should understand your schedule and not whine to you. If you do get 'guilted' by people, you may have to discuss it with them directly. Otherwise you may be tempted to increase the distance and drop them from your life, which is not always the best thing unless you truly have nothing in common. Regardless of how busy you are, don't even think of missing out on any kind of birthday celebration with your closest friends. If understanding the importance of birthdays isn't the difference between female friendships and male–female romances, then we don't know what is. If you are lucky enough to be in love with a cultured and stylish man, then it is natural to want to spend every waking and non-waking moment in his arms. But that would be teenage behaviour. You can be forgiven if you are in obsessive mode for the first month, but then it's time for fresh air. Instead, practise restraint and force yourself to see your other friends *sans* lover. You will benefit from seeing your friends to go shopping or for drinks; try not to gloat too much about new love, especially if you are the only one in a relationship. Be sensitive: some of your close friends may be very lonely or going through a horrible break-up. Be there for them. You know they'll be there for you.

Troubleshooting

Crisis management is an FG speciality. When she has a life-defining moment, whether it is losing a job, a parent or a lover, then support must be offered immediately by her circle. The words 'I don't know what to say' do not exist in the FG's vocabulary. The essential skill, one which every FG possesses, is knowing when the friend in need wants her input or simply needs a shoulder to cry on. In most cases, listening, not speaking, is what is required. The wounded party might want to rant or just to sit quietly, so follow her lead and avoid prying questions like 'Did you really steal money from work?' and 'Is he seeing someone else?' But be sincerely outraged on her behalf when she tells you that Bingo is now with Fifi.

Of course, if her friend does solicit her advice, an FG rolls up her sleeves and gets down to a full-on strategy session. She calls on her own experience (vast and comprehensive) to help her friend solve the crisis at hand. She offers her friend a place to crash if home is lonely, offers to call other friends to notify them of the situation, sends flowers or takes the friend drinking (but sees her home) so that she may truly cry it out.

These are all reasonable expectations of best friends. But be aware that even a caring FG has limits. If you are the heartbroken person, then of course you need your friends, but there is a two-week statute of limitations on crying on their shoulders on a daily basis. After those two weeks, it's time to change the subject – not permanently, but you must begin to show that you've got a grip and are trying to move on. A wise manoeuvre would be to spread the ex-boyfriend grief around to a few friends so that everyone gets a break and you benefit from fresh ears. Beyond a fortnight, you become difficult to be around and you lose sympathy.

FGs *like Gilt not Guilt*

Because FGs care about doing the right thing at all times, they are easily manipulated by guilt. It is not, however, their own modus operandi. Issues of guilt can become sticky when friendships are in flux. If a friendship seems to be changing and you are not spending the time together that you used to, it may be that it has run its course.

No-one likes to think that their friendship is unwanted, but as people mature and their careers develop they may lose touch with old friends who no longer share common ground. You must remember that some women are simply busier than others. Your friend could love you dearly but not have the spare time she used to. Do not demand more than she is willing to give. By nagging or calling frequent attention to the differences in your availability, you will only make your time together seem like a duty, and that's no fun for either of you. To assess your status, invite the friend out and give her the opportunity to choose the time and place. In person you will either have the same good old time as if you'd seen each other just the other day, or you'll be struggling for laughs and she will beat an early retreat.

Often it will happen that your closest friends work in the same field as you do. This can cause some feelings of jealousy and guilt when your social calendar is filled with coveted parties and dinners. Are you obliged to invite your friend when you know she's dying to meet the people you know? This can be tricky and requires a Fabulous Girl to be completely honest with herself. If you are not threatened by your friend in any way (i.e. she doesn't want your job), then it would be polite to invite her if it is appropriate – say, a house party or media event. Obviously this is not the case if the occasion is an intimate dinner party; you are not obliged to extend the invitation in this case, though it would be a generous and thus fabulous approach to friendship.

The issue of spending more time with one friend than another can also arise. If, for example, your two closest friends and you do many things together, but during one whimsical afternoon you and only one of them spotted a fab clothing sale and decided to go shopping, are you required to invite the third friend along on this jaunt? No – all three of you are entitled to girl time away from the others. A shopping spree, tea or movie should not raise the hackles of the left-out friend. In the case of couple friends, you should also feel free to break up groupings of couples when entertaining. If you and your boyfriend socialize an awful lot with two other couples, you aren't obliged to have them over only in that configuration every time. Everyone likes a change, and this shouldn't be the source of bad feeling.

Ending Friendships

The break-up of a friendship is the hardest break-up of all. When you want to end a romantic relationship, you know what to do, right? 'I'm sorry, but I just don't feel the same way any more and I think we should stop seeing each other.' For some reason this is simply unthinkable in platonic relationships. Ending a friendship is one of those situations in which an indirect approach is best. The rather cold, just-stop-returning-their-calls technique never fails. Another thing you absolutely must do is stop yourself from uttering that knee-jerk phrase 'We should get together', which will inevitably fall from your lips when talking to a friend. Friends, of course, will say it, and to this we suggest delaying tactics. Never apologize for being busy or unavailable; simply say, 'That day is no good for me, I've got plans.' Do not offer alternative dates. When you can't come up with an excuse and have to get together, why not invite along a few school chums or pals from the milieu in which you met? That way you can at least talk about the times when you had more in common.

More Money

Bound as it is to success and worth, money can be a tricky issue for friends to navigate. Whether one pal suddenly hits the jackpot or was simply born with a silver spoon in her mouth, a discrepancy in income can be awkward.

As the poor cousin in the equation, you must not assume that your wealthier friend wants to make up the difference when you go out together. Always look after your half of the bill even if she's got more than enough to cover the whole thing. You'll both feel more like equal partners in your friendship by handling shares expenses this way.

If it's you who has the bigger bank balance, the onus to be sensitive is even greater. While you may feel like treating your poorer pals all the time, be careful not to make them feel like charity cases. But also be sensitive when choosing dinner spots. Ask them to pick so they won't feel awkward when a too-big bill arrives on the table.

Gift-giving among friends can be a manners minefield. While everyone adores receiving presents, some people are more grateful for the effort than others. Even for your closest friend, you can sometimes choose a gift she doesn't like. Don't take it personally. You can tell by your friend's facial expression if your gift was enjoyed or not. If it wasn't, then offer to exchange it. FGs are such smart shoppers that they know to keep receipts! If you have been given the world's ugliest clock, for instance, and your friend is asking if you like the gift, you must tell the truth and say that it's not your style – unless the giver is ranting on about the girl-hours it took to pick it out or the hassles of shipping the hideous thing from Istanbul, in which case, unfortunately, it is best to bite it and say thanks. Remember, it's the thought, not what's been bought, that counts.

NEVER A BORROWER NOR A LENDER BE AN FG…

Borrowing money is solely the territory of best friends. Even then, it should only be done under dire circumstances and preferably when you have guaranteed money coming in for short-term payback. Try to make the request reasonable – under £250 – unless your friend is a millionaire multimedia mogul.

No matter how liquid your friend is, set terms for repayment with interest. The friend may choose to waive the interest, but that is her prerogative, not yours. When the money is due or close to due, you should make a point of reminding your friend that you have not forgotten and will get her the money. If you are still short of cash, don't hide it: tell her. It is a grand gesture of rudeness to borrow money and then not acknowledge it due to continued insolvency. Forcing the lender to bring up the loan is poor form. Trust us, she remembers but is waiting for you to mention it.

If, however, you have loaned money and the calendar has swept past the date of payment by at least two weeks, employ a subtle approach first. Simply ask the borrower how she is doing, if things are improving since that talk a few months back; she should take the hint. If not, you may have to say directly, 'I hate to ask, but I could do with that £250 back when you can.'

Soap Dish

Dishing out personal information should be akin to a five-course meal spread out over time. Facts such as place of birth, college attended and what you do for a living are definitely appetizer material. However, revealing that you are currently under the guidance of a psychiatrist (which many an FG will be at least once in her life) is certainly the fruit and cheese plate. If you are on the receiving end of such openness, be gracious and understanding. However, you do not have to commiserate if it makes you uncomfortable. You're not obliged to make confessions because someone else is. In this situation, it is not rude to be evasive. Your interest in the other person will be your gauge to how much you want to reveal.

THINGS THAT SHOULDN'T BE ASKED

In this tell-all age, it's a necessary reminder that personal questions should not be asked until you are beginning to know someone well. This isn't to say you can't be friendly and warm to someone you have just met, but you should save both your curiosity and your insights into her life until you have known a person for some time – no inquisitions into her childhood or parents, her income or what kind of plastic surgery she has had.

If you have made an enquiry that seems not to be warmly received, back off immediately. It's not your right to know the intimate details of someone else's life before she wants you to.

Relationships and Friendships

There is nothing more grand than being freshly in love. But if you're still a fabulously single girl, then watching your best girlfriend wax rhapsodic about the latest trinket Bingo bought her or their upcoming February getaway to Martinique is about as much fun as liposuction (only you get less out of it). This is where the FG trait of graciousness comes into play. Of course you must tell your friend how 'completely happy' you are for her and you must not complain when you are cast aside during that first month of new-couple bliss. Whining that you never see your friend any more will only cause her to want to see you even less. Instead you must endure seeing her with him more often than not and swallow your pride if you become the third wheel on their movie or dinner dates. After all, your friend is taking your feelings into consideration by inviting you along. This, too, can be too much of a good thing for all three of you. Try suggesting that you and your girlfriend go for weekly girl drinks or dinner and gracefully bow out of the couple dates. And take heart: perhaps Bingo has handsome single male friends.

MATCHMAKING

This is the temptation of every happy-in-love girl. But it is utterly wrong to push your friend into blind dates or double dates with Bingo's best buddy Bob unless she expresses a direct inclination to do so. You definitely don't want your single girlfriend to feel like you think there's something wrong with her singleness. Sometimes an FG relishes her singledom and does not want to be trapped in a relationship just so she can see her girlfriend more often. If you are happily coupled but your best friend is happily single, try to prise yourself away from your beau to spend time with her. You'll need it when your affair reaches the twilight stage or worse. Pushing friends aside is never fabulous behaviour and may make you a fair-weather friend.

If, however, your single friend is looking for love, it's perfectly fine to orchestrate situations where she will meet new people, and hey, if one of them happens to be a single man... just don't make it too obvious. If you're having a bunch of people around for drinks, invite your friend as well as George from accounting. If they hit it off, great; if not, no-one feels embarrassed or uncomfortable.

I HATE MY BEST FRIEND'S MAN

The idiot makes a rude, stupid joke loud enough for the entire restaurant to not enjoy. You try to hide behind the menu, exchanging looks with your best friend only to discover she's laughing. Then you sigh and realize: you hate her boyfriend. The only problem is, she doesn't – she loves the lout. What does she see in him? You shouldn't concern yourself with this question – that is, if you want to remain friends.

It is very bad to criticize a friend's mate unless you are expressly asked for your opinion. Even then, tread cautiously. If your wisdom has been requested and it's a new courtship, try 'He's a smart bloke, very strong opinions'. If the relationship is in trouble, you can be a little more forthright. 'I'm sure he means well, but he can be obnoxious. You might talk to him about curbing his unedited diatribes.' And if it's over and you want it to stay that way, you can say, 'I think you made the right choice.' If you truly speak your mind – 'Thank God you're not with him any more. I don't know how you could stand him. You're much too good for him' – then of course the damage is done: she'll end up married to the cad and never forgive you for being honest.

The inevitable will occur, and you will gradually see less and less of your friend. Better to try and prise her away from couple bliss for girl time.

SHE HATES YOUR MAN

You probably know it. Even if she's trying to be polite about it, you can probably tell if your close friend really dislikes your boyfriend. This can obviously be a very awkward situation, but it needn't be the end of the world.

If you're at the very beginning of a relationship, take a moment to consider the possibility that your friend might be seeing something you don't see. And isn't her judgement usually exactly right? You may realize at the end of your romance that your pal was right all along about how controlling Bingo is.

But you may also be dealing with a friend who does not easily make new acquaintances – in fact, the two of you might have taken some time to warm up to each other. In this case, let it ride. She may just be feeling a little jealous that most of your free time is going to the new lover and not to her.

If you are in a romance that you have no intention of getting out of, you need to make some decisions about your pal's feelings (and the expressions of those feelings). It's easy enough to organize your time with her away from your man. If her bias makes itself more apparent – say, in the form of intentionally mispronouncing his name – then you are absolutely justified in telling her to knock it off. Let her know that while she has every right to her opinion, her behaviour is hurting your feelings and your friendship with her.

Fair-Weather Friends

Fair-weather friends are not friends: they are support free-loaders. You know the type – they only call you when they need something or have been dumped and want someone to introduce them to new men. But when you called them after you were fired or the cleaners ruined your Chanel dress, all you received was a 'Can I call you right back?' and that was three weeks ago. This type of girl is only happy when she's with a man, and when she's not, she just wants girlfriends as a dating service. Fortunately, this is the type of friendship that is most easy to end. On the rare occasion when she does telephone and you start to hear the old tune playing again, then don't return her call. That's right, politely tell her you're really busy.

Kill the Messenger: Gossip

Everyone, but everyone, does it. After all, gossip is fun. And although nobody likes to think about themselves as the subject of gossip, you know you are, right? This contradiction presents the need for the 'kill the messenger' rule. If Bingo lets slip that Fifi thinks your clothes are blah and your opinions obtuse, you'll feel hurt by Fifi. But it will also taint your feelings for Bingo. Why does he want you to be hurt? Thus the rule: never pass gossip on to its target. If you have friends who can't seem to shake the habit of passing on nasty comments others have made about you, it's time to get tough. If this is the friend's only flaw, tell her you want her to keep her gloomy news to herself from now on. Who knows, maybe she's got some twisted sense of loyalty. It's also likely, how-ever, that on some level this friend wants you to be brought down a notch by hearing what other people think of you –

very badly played. Are these the actions of friends? We think not.

However, there are exceptions. There you are on a beautiful Thursday afternoon, skipping work and eating takeaway sushi in the park. Then you spot them: a happy-in-love couple holding hands and laughing. Seems your best friend's husband is also skiving – from your best friend! The age-old dilemma whirls through your mind. Yes, your friend needs to know; on the other hand, remember the 'kill the messenger' rule. Some close friends have prior agreements on this subject. If you don't, your first course of action is to confront the cheater, not in the park, but as soon as possible. Of course it is what it looks like, but at least you can tell yourself you gave him a chance to explain how he loves his cousin Mabel so much he needs to nibble her earlobes. It's perfectly correct to force his hand: 'It's you or it's me, but someone's going to tell her.'

Compliments, on the other hand, should always be passed on to their subjects. And the same goes for serious concerns for your pal's well-being, as in, 'I saw your job advertised in an internal memo!'

Three Musketeers?

The politesse of three close friends needs to be handled gently. If, as in the above situation, your friend Alice's boyfriend is having an affair, only it turns out to be with the third point in the friend triangle, Beatrice, you need to do some serious manoeuvring. Forget about merely confronting the lout; you need to sit down with Beatrice and ask what is going on.

If you are stuck in the middle, there is nothing you can do that will be right in both Alice's and Beatrice's minds.

Beatrice should do everything in her power to keep you out of it. You have every right to tell Beatrice you don't want to hear about it. And when it does hit the fan – and it always does – you can definitely insist that the subject is off limits.

Your loyalty to both friends is tested here, and if Beatrice decides to not inform Alice of what she's been up to, then a less sticky and less confrontational approach would be to tell lesser friend Deirdre who you know can't keep a secret and let her do your bidding. Then watch out: you will be hearing about the betrayal from both sides.

This inter-friend boyfriend-sharing is a rarity. A more common problem occurs when two of the three friends are present and the conversation turns to the third. It is natural to complain about the absent friend, but try to not say anything that you wouldn't say directly to her face given the right circumstances. If your criticism cannot be spoken in that manner, then the absent friend is not a true friend. Of course life sometimes throws up bad circumstances that can divide friendships over short periods of time (for months or even years), but then patience is your weapon.

Another troublesome truth of the FG threesome is that you hear opposing opinions on separate occasions. Alice insists that Beatrice despises your new hair colour; Beatrice is outraged when confronted. She argues that Alice got it all wrong and that what she actually said was that she would despise your aubergine shade on *her*. Who do you believe? Chances are you'll never know for sure who said what, but you may want to consider going back to brunette – after all, these are your friends. Some threesome friends decide it is best to never discuss the third member of the troika in her absence.

Married Friends and Their Little Angels

There are many rites of passage for the Fabulous Girl. One major one, of course, is marriage. We will talk about an FG's wedding in another chapter; here we deal only with the single FG coping with her friend's marriage after the fact. It is a sad reality that a close friend's marriage will forever alter the friendship. The bond is altered by her new bond with her husband. She just won't be available any more for cruising the menswear department at Selfridges or for three-hour chat fests on Saturday night, at least not with the frequency you're used to. An FG will feel the absence intensely. It will be a shock when your conversation shifts from make-up to mortgages. Some subjects will come up that you never thought worth mentioning:

1. Pensions and savings plans
2. The merits of buying over renting a flat
3. Mortgage rates
4. Income tax
5. The declining sex life of your married friend
6. Everything the new husband does wrong
7. How you should join her in wedded bliss
8. Entertaining or visiting in-laws
9. How you need more focus in your life
10. How career isn't the most important thing in life

There is little sense in complaining about the change in the friendship. It's a done deal. Better to accept that everyone in a social circle needs to remain flexible as you all go through various life shifts.

Eventually your friend's newlywed-head will clear and you will resume 'girl nights'. Beware, though: she may grow to envy your freedom and you to envy her stability. Your break-ups and affairs may become more threatening to your married friends than to your fellow single women. You will have to expand your friendship base in order to spend time with other single FGs as the discussions you'll need to have about men and dating will be less understood by your married mates. It's as though marriage makes many women forget what singledom is like – they try, but they can't quite remember.

PREGNANCY

As with weddings, it is important for parents-to-be and their families to remember that it is only they who feel the world has changed with their news. For the rest of the world, it is business as usual. The rest of the world will be far happier for you, by the way, if you are not shoving your bliss down its throat. It's understandable for expectant couples to forget everything else except their bundles-to-be, but manners, after all, are about thinking of others. The pregnant FG will build up many more points for not talking about it every waking second, not talking as if she were the first woman to ever find herself pregnant, doing her best not to terrorize those around her. The smallest effort in this direction will be heralded by your friends and family as extremely brave and cool. A word of good taste is necessary here too: aside from parents and grandparents of the future child, no-one is interested in seeing the ultrasound. Please keep the image in the family.

Quivering in the wake of an expectant mother is something the loyal FG must endure. Despite the rumours, not all pregnant women are happy with their new 'glow'. If your friend is hormonal and sensitive you may witness or hear the following:

1. You mention work; she mentions how she misses work.

2. You get a promotion; she stares at the floor and mutters, 'That's great.'

3. You squeeze into sample sale outfits; she won't enter the store.

4. You ask her how she's feeling; she snaps, 'How do you think? Fat and ugly!'

5. You mention something you read about babies; she reminds you that you wouldn't know a thing about it.

6. You're still dating and laughing about it; she announces she wants a divorce.

Avoid these surefire temper boosters:

1. Wow, are you big!

2. What do you do all day?

3. Is the baby's room finished?

4. I plan on having a child when I'm more financially able.

5. Did you consider a nanny?

Of course, many women love being pregnant! They are a pleasure to be with, and an FG will look forward to the fun of shopping for baby, helping choose colours for rooms and maybe even babysitting.

Lots of pregnant women strive to remain the fun-loving gals they were before getting knocked up. The rest of the world may assume that a pregnant woman is public property, so support her efforts at maintaining autonomy. Don't assume they don't want to meet you at your favourite bar. Don't assume they don't want a drink either. Don't ask her if that coffee is a decaf. Don't assume that the coming baby is the only thing she wants to talk about.

THE BLESSED EVENT

Unless the baby is a relative or you are a birthing coach, you do not have to be at the hospital for the birth. The parents will call when they can and then you can make your journey to the hospital. Make it brief – all involved will be exhausted.

Ask what your friend needs; you may be thinking flowers, but she may be craving pastrami on rye.

Once the child has been brought home, try cooking a reheatable meal for the busy couple. This will take a load of stress off them. And, during the first two weeks of the new-born's life, keep your visits short.

HAPPY FIRST BIRTHDAY

This often poses a dilemma, though for an FG it should not be. There is no reason on earth why a child-free person should feel obliged to attend a one-year-old's birthday party. Most of the attendees will be family or other parents. No-one else with a life could find such a gathering remotely interesting. If your friend-turned-mum insists on inviting you, you can either make up an excuse or endure one drink and bring a gift. If she is an FG, she will rightly tell you that there is a party but that she completely understands why you won't be coming.

Some FGs do go out of their way to combine baby birth-day parties with adult fun. A barbecue at which kids can tear around the garden and adults can drink and enjoy the sun is a good example of a party that parents and non-parents can both enjoy.

Unless both the new mum and the child-free FG are will-ing to be flexible, babies can be a serious obstacle to maintaining friendship in the early years. A child-free FG can no longer expect her pal with kids to drop everything and run off to a matinee. And if you have kids, you can't expect that your child-free friends want to see your whole family every time you spend time together.

Of course we're not saying you won't still be friends, but rest assured that you will see even less of each other. Your friend will be constantly tired, thoroughly and justly caught up in raising a child. If she's a working mum, then she has even less flexibility. Once again, that dual jealousy over freedom versus family can set in. Deciding if and when to have a child is a decision every FG must make at some point in her life. Having a friend who makes the decision before you can be an excellent opportunity for you to have a close-up look at what motherhood is really like.

Stalking and Other Bad Ideas

There are occasions when an FG or her best FG girlfriend go over the edge of well-played decorum – for example, becoming obsessed with a lover, an ex or a one-night stand. While an FG will tolerate endless conversations about the obsession, she should not indulge the following requests:

1. Do not take the obsessed by the home of the object of her obsession to see if he's at home or alone;

2. Calling said object from your phone on behalf of friend and hanging up if he answers;

3. Asking acquaintances probing questions on behalf of friends regarding object;

4. Arranging to 'run into' object with intention of bringing up friend's name to gauge reaction.

Other bad ideas include:

1. Shoplifting, even if it seems easy and fun;

2. Destroying or damaging property of ex or ex's new gal;

3. Cutting each other's hair, unless FG is a stylist.

Men Friends

The Fabulous Girl will have a long list of male friends – be they ex-boyfriends, platonic pals or men who wish they were the boyfriend. Male friends are an important part of a well-balanced social diet.

CHAPSTICKS

For the single girl, 'Chapsticks' (those platonic chaps who stick by you through thick and thin) make great escorts to events. They are also there to shoulder the burden of sex during break-ups, crushes who won't call and bitter fights with boyfriends. It is natural that some of the Chapsticks will have a lingering crush on an FG, and she will know this. It may never be acknowledged except perhaps for one burst of affection from him, but the sexual undercurrent will be ever-present. While this is flattering, using Chapsticks as back-ups is not kind. If a male friend's affection is long-suffering, then running to him every time your cad Bingo dumps you will be torture for him and you will eventually push him away. If you are blissfully in love and are having great sex, the Chapstick will not enjoy hearing the details, so don't give them. Benefit from the Chapstick's insight into male libido and thought processes only if he is not 'secretly' in love with you. Then reap the rewards of having your own spy.

MARRIED MEN AS BUDDIES

Eventually a Chapstick will get married, and quite frankly, some women can't stand their boyfriends, let alone their husbands, having close female friends. However, as an FG you want everyone to adore you and cannot fathom why the new wife feels threatened by little ol' you. It is important to respect the newlyweds' boundaries regarding friends of the opposite sex. The married man should know the edge he walks more clearly than anyone, so follow his lead in terms of the frequency and nature of your hanging out.

When you do see his wife, though, make a point of showing interest in her as well. If you are getting the cold shoulder from his missus, then maybe all is not as well as he says. Unless you are in fact making out in the back of your Beetle, though, a wife's green eye is something they need to discuss between themselves. Engaging him in conversation about his wife's feelings of jealousy is a subtle form of flirtation. If you feel compelled to do this, your motives are the ones that need pondering.

FUCK BUDDIES

Having one or two fuck buddies in her little red book is essential in the life of an FG. Think of them as Chapsticks Plus. A fuck buddy is the guy that you'd never dream of getting serious with and he, likewise, doesn't see you that way. He will come by 'for a drink' like a trouper. Sex with a fuck buddy can be great and will often run towards the athletic and enthusiastic variety. But fuck buddies can also be tender since they're not worried that affection will be read by you as commitment.

However flexible the fuck buddy is, he may have to be redefined when an FG finds herself in a committed relationship. It is possible to remain friends; as with most fuck buddies, his role is on and off. If you are suddenly a taken woman, then you must explain to your fuck buddy that sex is now off-limits. Eventually your significant other may sniff out that fuck buddy Bingo is exactly that and ask the question. 'Have you ever slept with Bingo?' How confident and secure your relationship is will determine if your beau can be trusted with the truth. Likewise, make sure your fuck buddy can keep your secret to himself.

The Fabulous Girl's Perfect Day Shopping with her Best FG

9.30 a.m.
Rise after an extra-long beauty rest. A light but energy-boosting breakfast.
Wardrobe: White or flesh-tone thong, button-up shirt, skirt and flat shoes.
Grooming: Shower, full hair and make-up.
Fabulous Girl Tip: A watch is your only accessory.

11.00 a.m.
Meet best friend at the nicest shopping district in town. Try on lots of clothes whether or not you intend or can afford to buy anything.
Fabulous Girl Tip: Try on clothes pre-lunch to ensure a flat stomach.

1.30 p.m.
Ladies Who Lunch: Tablecloths and waiter service.
Table Talk: Gossip, fashion, men, goals.
Fabulous Girl Tip: No fast food.

2.30–4.00 p.m.
Après-lunch: Giving the 'maybes' a second look.
Manicures, pedicures, flicking through magazines, shoe-shopping.
Fabulous Girl Tip: Swollen feet guarantee fit.

4.00–5.00 p.m.
Tea, read, nap.

5.00 p.m.

Unpack.
Private fashion show.
Remove tags and put away new threads.
Fabulous Girl Tip: Revel in your good taste.

I knocked on Missy's door at around 11.30 that night, when I knew she'd be home from her shift. She opened the door in her bedtime things – boxer shorts to her knees and a Cambridge sweatshirt. I broke into our old song, 'Sweatshirt souvenirs...that's all I have left of him...'

'Hello.' She wasn't laughing let alone singing along with me. 'I was just about to go to bed, but come in.'

We were off to a bad start. Of course I should have called her instead of just showing up. I suppose I thought she would put me off. As we walked up the stairs to her kitchen, I tried to remember which former lover's sweatshirt went missing for Missy's pyjamas. I think it was about three exes ago. Missy had been so hung up on him. For about a month after they split up, she made me call him from the phone box on the corner to see if a woman answered. When a woman did start answering regularly, we found out he'd moved to New York. To get married.

While Missy made tea, I was feeling like a big person for waiting for her to apologize for her recent bad behaviour.

'All right, Miss Thing, what's up?' I said eventually.

'What are you talking about?'

'OK, let's be adults, all right?' I steadied myself against the counter. 'You're obviously angry about something and I don't know what, so why don't we just get it over with?'

'People change. And it's all great. I mean, it's mostly

Eleanor.' I had no idea what Missy was talking about, but it didn't stop me from wanting to shift whatever aggravation she was feeling for me over to Eleanor so much that I nearly replied, 'Yeah, Eleanor, what a bitch.'

Instead I nodded. Missy continued. 'And she's probably going to marry that idiot and have babies and you'll probably move to Paris and be all rich and successful and all that is just fine but I'll, like, still be here in this flat and working at the restaurant. And I'll never see either of you. Which is kind of what it's like now, anyway.'

'Well, you don't have to keep living in this flat,' I offered. 'Where do you want to live?'

'Funny.'

'I just mean that you should do whatever you want to do, Missy. Do you think you might know...'

'Nope.'

We both nodded. The phone rang. Missy rolled her eyes. 'That'll be Caroline. She's been there for six months and still doesn't understand how to cash up. Hello? El? Hello, El? Are you on your mobile? She sounds terrible, I think she's in a cab. Eleanor. OK, just come over.'

'We broke up.'

'Again.' I raised my eyebrows at Missy. She went down the hall and put the kettle on to make a fresh pot. 'What happened?' I patted Eleanor's shoulder.

'He thinks that we rely on each other too much. That we don't inspire each other to grow.' She blew her nose hard. In the kitchen, while Missy and I were fetching mugs and the teapot, I whispered, 'I think he's seeing someone else. He's back on the growing thing again.'

'That fucker.' Missy reserved this word for the very bad. 'I don't know if I can go through this again with her,' she whispered back.

I reached in the cupboard for the chocolate-dipped shortbread. 'I know, but just remember what happened to me last time.'

'Well, so much for my theory about marriage and babies. That was a bit stupid.'

'Maybe a bit. Come on, let's deal with it.'

Sex and Courtship

When you're only seeing someone at the weekend he is not your boyfriend. You can say that you're seeing him or that you're sleeping with him, but if you don't see him on a Wednesday he is definitely not your boyfriend. That was what I was telling myself about Felix. Because I knew that I was too old to be with a musician. Way too old. And that was why I confined it to the weekends. There was no way I could keep his hours during the week. I could barely keep them on a Saturday.

Missy called just when I was putting my coat on.

'Where is it tonight? The Elmo?'

'No, they're playing at the Horseshoe. But they're only opening tonight, so I'm hoping to drag him away by midnight. I'm not sure I can do brunch tomorrow...it depends on if we end up at this drinking club or whatever.'

'Whatever is right. You've missed three brunches, young lady. Have a good time.'

I came out of the newsagent next to the bar and saw him. My stomach jumped. Would he remember me? Or would he only remember being splashed with Scotch?

'Hey! How are you?' He put a very firm hand on my elbow and left it there.

'Hi. I'm so sorry about the spilling thing, so stupid...'

'I'm not sorry,' he said, his hand still firm. I tried to think of a witty remark. But none came. Maybe Groovy·and I had nothing to say to each other.

'I hear you're making a film?' I asked, hoping to have landed on the appropriate way to describe it. Maybe you're supposed to say 'director' or 'filmmaker'.

'Well, it looks like it. The possibility for disaster and financial ruin still lingers, though. But we may start shooting next month.'

'That's great.'

We both laughed at nothing.

'Baaaabe.' An arm around my waist now, not so firm. Groovy Guy dropped his grip on me. Felix put his face against my ear and sort of licked and kissed and scratched it. 'We're finished. But you've got to hear this next band. They rock. Hey, I'm Felix.' He stuck his thin, white arm out at G.G. 'You should come in too.'

'Thanks, I've got to head home. You two have fun.'

It wasn't smooth, but I had to act fast. I stuck a hand in my bag, fished out a business card from the bottom of it and slipped it into G.G.'s shirt pocket. He raised his eyebrows. 'So, call me about that thing. I'd love to hear more about that project,' I said.

He nodded, smiled and frowned all at once and walked off, thinking God-knows-what about my business-card manoeuvre. It was my first time, so I'd probably been a bit awkward.

'Ready, babe?' I looked at Felix and thought about how nice he really was and felt a little guilty that I wouldn't be sleeping with him any more. I know it's not polite to reduce people to type, but once your brain has just gone ahead and done it with a particular person, it's a strong signal to keep your clothes on in their presence from then on. I found myself thinking, 'Oh, you're the last musician I'm going to ever sleep with. Well, that's that, then.'

* * *

'Missy, come on! He might notice us parked here,' I groaned.

'Just a few minutes longer. The lights are on, he's bound to walk by the window, then I'll know.'

'We've got better things to do,' whined Eleanor.

The three of us were in my car outside the studio of a commercial photographer Missy had slept with a few times. Even though she had stolen the standard sweatshirt, she was still hooked on him. She was stalking him. And now all of us were: triple-stalking, a crime of passion and humiliation. Finally the object of her desire strolled by the window. And he wasn't alone. He and his buddy were both naked. And didn't seem to care if anyone could see them.

'He's sleeping with Ralph!' Missy was horrified.

'I guess you just don't have what it takes,' I retorted.

Eleanor and I were laughing so hard I ground the gears as I drove away.

'Really, it's fine. It happens to everyone. And I'm happy just to lie here with you anyway.' I had my hand on his chest and was pulling gently on the curly hairs there.

He sighed deeply. 'I know I said my marriage was over. But yesterday we decided to try again.'

The signs had been there: not being allowed to call him at home, meeting in dark places in far-flung neighbourhoods, not to mention the hotel room we were in. I had met Married Guy a month earlier during what I thought was his separation. I thought I belonged with a mature, established lover who knew what he wanted.

'I'm so sorry. This isn't fair to you, I know.' He started to get up and pull on his shirt.

'You said you were filing for divorce.' It's not that I wanted to marry him myself, but a girl has a right to the facts.

'I'll ring you in a couple of days, alright?' He looked around for his socks, which had rolled under the bed.

'Mmm. I don't think so. I'll let you pay for the hotel, though.'

'Of course.'

That was my one experience with a married man. I was determined not to let it ruin whatever optimism I still had about relationships. But running into the cads of this world can really get you down.

Sex and Courtship

In the name of decorum, we have chosen to combine these two subjects into one chapter. For in the world of Fabulous Girl, which comes first, sex or dating, may change as often as her lipstick.

The role of sex in the life of the Fabulous Girl is very different from the one it played in her mother's or grandmother's day. The FG is a liberal woman and is not afraid to pursue sex just for the pleasure of it. Having many lovers or only a few is a choice that no longer has dire consequences for her 'reputation'. The FG understands that sex can mean everything or nothing; she can have sex with a stranger or with her best friend. No-one but the FG herself decides what place sex holds in the personal hierarchy of her life. But she has few role models to look to for manners in the bedroom. This chapter offers sage advice on sexual etiquette that will serve to enhance the FG's sex life and to abate confusion and frustration between the sexes. Despite our culture's calling an open season on sex, there is a polite and civilized way to enjoy the carnal pleasures.

Of course the FG can have sex without commitment, but

what if she wants to find someone special? One word that can send shivers down the spine of even the most fabulous of Fabulous Girls is 'dating'. That state between blissfully single and in-couple is fraught with anxiety, self-doubt and frustration. But this girl does not despair! She invented the art of courtship and knows how to get what she wants – and further, how to discourage those she doesn't want.

The Art of Flirting

Flirting is a very important part of being an FG – not to mention a useful member of your social scene. Everyone loves a flirt because a flirt makes those around her feel sexy – men and women alike. Remember, though, that this is your purpose: to make people feel good. Your purpose is not to make Bingo think he's going to score when there's no chance in hell that he'll ever see you naked. Similarly it's not cool to make another woman feel you're out to poach her man. So, keep it light and keep your hands to yourself. 'You look so handsome in that shade of blue' will leave him feeling chuffed. But say 'Men in leather make me really hot', and everyone feels nervous.

An FG is always aware of her own motivations. Are you trying to annoy that girl over there by making eyes at her boyfriend? Is it really very nice to flirt with a guy who you know pines for you? Are you intentionally making your boyfriend jealous because he was half an hour late to pick you up tonight? (Actually, go ahead. Tardiness deserves punishment.)

There are signs that you've gone too far, for example, when he's standing too close to you and his girlfriend comes over and puts the 'He's mine, bitch' clamp on his arm. The ultimate sign that you are in fact an 'overboard' flirt is when the men around you keep their distance. Women will often be jealous of an FG in full flirt mode, but if the men in the room are raising eyebrows or avoiding you, then it's time to go subtle – think 'lipbalm' instead of 'lipstick'.

If you are flirting with a mind to taking things further, here are some ways to let him know it's not all innocent. Make prolonged eye contact. Only a second more than normal sends a powerful message and it's subtle enough that if you get the wrong response, you can back up with no loss of dignity. If all is going well, touch his elbow to emphasize a point. Make it clear that you are alone at the event, or with a girlfriend, or that you wouldn't mind hearing more about that fascinating trip of his to Napoli or Nepean – it doesn't really matter, does it? A delicate flourish at night's end is to surreptitiously slip your phone number into his palm or pocket. This is why a Fabulous Girl has a few calling cards on hand at all times.

Watching him flirt

Prone to jealousy? You need to give your date some leeway on this one and allow him some flirting space. It will make you more attractive to him if you don't flip out over every little thing. And remember, if he's paying too much attention to another woman, maybe you should be flirting with him more yourself. If he flirts excessively with other women even though he knows it makes you uncomfortable it might be that he is an inconsiderate creep!

First Dates

RITUALS OF ROMANCE

Nowadays, men and women don't always date in the traditional boy-asks-girl-to-dinner-and-a-movie kind of way. It is quite common to meet a member of the opposite sex who you are attracted to at a party or through friends. You strike up a conversation, there is chemistry and *voilà* – at the end of the evening, he asks you for your number or, more slyly, asks the hostess for your number.

No matter who makes the first call, a popular first date is daytime coffee. This is a very casual approach to courtship and is extremely noncommittal – as in, 'You're interesting, so let's meet again and continue our talk about Nasdaq' – compared with a dinner, which sends a very clear signal of real attraction. The reason for coffee is, of course, that we are all deeply afraid of rejection. Many of us feel uncomfortable letting our desires be known so early on. Coffee is easy. It lasts an hour, and then it's easy to beg off for other engagements should it not go well.

Another common first date is meeting for drinks. Once again you can keep it short and sweet, but it will be easier to make it clear that one of you is interested in more than simple conversation. Simply the extra effort one puts into grooming and wardrobe selection suggests a more acute level of attraction.

Dinner is second-date territory for all but the very bold. The intimate setting adds pressure but is a good test for compatibility of character (in quiet restaurants, awkward silences can resonate like shouts). At dinner the FG shines, because even if her date is a bore, she rises to the challenge and becomes the entertainment. And if all else fails, perhaps the waiter will be worth flirting with.

BEING ASKED AND ASKING

There will be occasions when an FG, being such a charmer, is asked out by the wrong man. Perhaps he's a nice guy but he just doesn't make your heart flutter. You must say no. Depending on his relation to your life (it could be you'll never see him again or it could be he's your best friend's brother), if you won't be meeting him again, a white lie is permissible. 'I'm already seeing someone' is the best response. If, however, he is in your circle of friends and thus can find out if you are single, then you may feel pressured to say 'Sure, sometime'. Instead, tell him that you are extremely busy and then ask for his number; do not give him yours. Then don't call him. If the man is persistent, then you may have to tell him that you see him only as a friend. This is usually enough discouragement.

An FG is brave enough to ask a man out. This may be terrifying, but many men love the novelty and boldness of it. This is a personal choice – some women hate the idea, others embrace being the 'aggressor'. You won't know which dynamic you prefer until you've sampled both. And yes, if you asked *him*, be prepared to pay for the two of you.

RECOVERING FROM BAD DATES
BUT STILL WANTING TO SEE HIM AGAIN

An FG can, every once in a while, blow her decorum. For instance, that first date with Mr Perfect is going swimmingly – they are sharing dinner at a Japanese restaurant and an FG does enjoy her sushi. Lucky for him, though, he opted for steak teriyaki. Lucky, because when you're at the cinema, you suddenly feel like death. That's right, you have food poisoning from that less-than-stellar futomaki. So you start vomiting in the Ladies and he's left sighing on the bench in the lobby.

He has to drive you home. If he really is Mr Perfect, he'll be understanding and nurturing, making sure you get into your lair in one piece but not hovering around to hear you being sick. Unfortunately, he may have to be Mr Perfect to get past your pallor and to think of kissing you after this initial encounter. And he should phone the next day to check you survived. If you wish to see him again, tell him. Be direct. Laugh at your disastrous date. If, however, you do not hear from him, then he is a cad and not worth knowing.

NOTES ON FOOD

There is nothing more distracting or embarrassing on a date than inappropriate food choices. An FG should learn to avoid particularly these foods when out with a new beau:

- Dim sum or sushi. These delicacies break off messily and are often left hanging out of your mouth. If you do manage to shove the food in, you may be left with chipmunk cheeks trying to chew more than you can swallow.
- Spaghetti, linguini, angel hair or other long stringy pasta.
- Sandwiches (unless at a cream tea).

The fundamental rule is never to order anything that cannot be eaten gracefully with a knife and fork. Even pizza should be carved, not bitten off, on early dates. This is also true of salad. Restaurants will often serve huge pieces of romaine or the like in a salad. Don't assume that everything is served bite-size, and that the extra-large leaf was meant to be shoved into your mouth whole because it came that way. Many fail to realize what a turn-off it is to watch a person contort and manoeuvre a head of lettuce into their mouth. Cutting lettuce into smaller bites is to be encouraged. If your date has poor table manners, example is the only weapon at your disposal: 'The rocket is so big that I have to use a knife...'

PROPER DATE BEHAVIOUR

When out on a date, whether the first or fifth, there are certain laws of decorum that must be strictly adhered to. One of the foremost signs of civility is the ability to look your date in the eye. Even if he is the most dreadful bore, you must give all the appearances of being thoroughly engaged by his talk on septic pumps. Your eye should not wander to a handsome waiter or to the TV hanging in the bar – though if he has taken you to a venue that airs round-the-clock sports, then you really shouldn't bother with him again.

If there are awkward pauses or silences, then ask him something about himself. He will never tire of talking on this subject.

Some women feel that it's not a date unless the man pays the bill. But as we've suggested, an FG is a modern woman and does not hold to these old-fashioned ideas. Usually. Who picks up the tab on those early dates can be tricky. If your suitor makes it clear that he'd like to take you out to dinner, then you can let him pay for the meal. When a man asks an FG out for an afternoon coffee or cocktails, it is not wrong to assume that he intends to pay for her. Nonetheless, an FG always carries some cash in case he's cheap. As unbelievable as it may sound, there are louts in dateland who may prise out a fiver from their wallets when the bill is only ten. Be prepared to pay, and then never go out with the cheapskate again.

Likewise, if you've asked someone out on a date, then you should be prepared to treat them. He may insist on paying the bill or at least his share of it. If he does this, then he is definitely trying to impress you and is also inclined towards taking a traditional male role in the courtship rituals. It's up to you whether this is a plus or a minus.

If it's not so clear and the two of you just made plans to get together, then an FG offers to pay half the bill. And once you're dating the same guy over time, you must definitely share the cost of going out or at the very least offer. You can't assume he makes more than you do just because he's a man, so why should he automatically pay for your dinner? If you do not intend to see him again, then you should definitely pay for your half of the bill. Of course, *you* know that paying for a meal doesn't mean anyone is obliged to offer themselves up as dessert later, but he might not.

An FG can be sure that a suitor is never going to make her happy if one or more of these things occur:

- He has a wandering eye for all the other women in the room.
- He keeps looking over your shoulder at the television at the bar.
- He never asks you about yourself and your career.
- He talks ill of his exes – all of them.
- He complains about the prices on the menu and cannot see value in nice things (e.g. five-star restaurants or designer clothing).
- He thinks you're just too fancy.
- He presses you to give him your home number when you're reluctant.
- He doesn't open the doors for you and doesn't say thank you when you do for him.
- He doesn't walk you to your car or ensure you get safely into a cab or bus.
- He keeps asking for details about your past relationships on the first date.
- He tells you about his stomach ailments or other infirmities.
- He hasn't made you laugh, not even once.

Post-First Date

The two of you chatted endlessly. He made you laugh: you made him swoon. You parted with a kiss on the cheek. Now what? You hope that if it was a truly successful date, the suitor (whoever asked the other out to begin with) may suggest getting together a second time. If you are confident you want to see the gent again, then tell him to call you.

Nonetheless, an FG does call or e-mail after a first date simply to say thank you.

If a few days go by and neither of you has contacted the other, then an FG should go ahead and make the call to see if a second date is even a possibility. This early dating ritual is a minefield, because if the gent does ask for a second date and the FG is really busy for a week or more, then he may feel inclined to believe she's disinterested. To avoid this, set a firm date for next time.

Cancelling a Date

If something comes up and you sincerely cannot make a date, call immediately; unless it's a car accident or the like, cancel a day in advance. Leaving it until he is waiting at the restaurant is only acceptable in true emergencies. If you're going to be late, then ask your date if he minds waiting rather than cancelling. If your date does not know you well, he may read the cancellation as a lack of interest.

When to Move from Supper to Sex

Of course, the one-night stand means the answer is immediately. A night of passion can lead to a relationship. But if you want a more traditional courtship, then having at least one or two dates beforehand is the norm. A drink as first date followed by dinner as second date can lead to sex on the third. If on the fifth date, an FG invites him over for dinner at her place, or vice versa, the evening is sure to involve sex. There are, however, other clear signs of impending passion.

INVITATION SUBTEXTS

In the land of dating, there exists a secret code. Before people know each other well enough to speak explicitly of their desires, this subtext takes the place of blunt language. From an etiquette perspective, the most important messages you need to decipher are those of a sexual nature – ways of saying 'This means sex' without saying it.

Code 1: 'Do you want to come in for a drink?'
This applies to a late-night after-dinner drink, not a more innocent pre-dinner cocktail, which may be consumed without sexual inference. Let's face facts: people have been substituting the word 'drink' for 'tonight's the night' for so long that anyone receiving such an invitation could justifiably assume they are being asked for a sleepover. It is very poor etiquette (and potentially dangerous) to extend this invitation if you don't mean to have sex. Conversely, a wise person declines such a loaded libation if all they want is a drink. If you're only after another round, far better to stay in the bar.

Code 2: 'Let's go away for the weekend.'
This particular invitation is crystal clear. If you're renting a hotel room, chances are there will be one bed and it will be king-size. It is the height of ill manners to accept his invitation to the country – or worse, a plane ticket to Belize – and

then spurn all advances. What did you think the hotel room was for, bowling? If you want to go on a platonic trip, say so beforehand and definitely pay your way.

Code 3: 'Why don't you come for a visit?'
This is a different matter. If you are visiting someone in another city and your relationship is unclear, requesting a guest room in their home is appropriate. And not at all definitive. Even if there is sexual tension, the host in such a scenario would be wise to assume separate sleeping arrangements – all the more fun should lust take its course.

Caveat: of course sex is never totally obligatory. If in any of these situations (and despite the best lustful intentions) you have a last-minute, non-strategic change of heart, backing out is fine. But a sincere apology – for the wound to your date's pride – is in order.

If none of the above invitations occur, then the challenge of 'bringing him home' needs to be addressed.

You may have been doing a good deal more than nuzzling in the back of the cab, but when he's watching you unlock your front door for the first time, you need to slow things down. If the man in question is someone you've been dating for a while, then what's another half an hour? You'll be more relaxed for the big moment if you make time for quiet romance now. And if you've only just met Bingo, then this interlude is critical. You may suddenly have a change of heart, and convincing him that you only meant to give him a drink, not an all-access pass, is easier if everyone is still dressed.

Of course, we strongly recommend that you do not bring a man home for a drink in the wee hours unless you intend to have sex with him. You may have made it explicitly clear that you are only offering a cocktail. But inviting a man into your home late at night with no intention of having sex with him, you risk two things: putting yourself in danger (if you are in the presence of a bad guy), and being impolite and hurtful (if you are in the presence of a nice guy).

If you're clear that it is sex you're after, then by all means proceed. Let's just do it with style and grace, shall we?

For those with flatmates, running the living-room gauntlet can be a bit tricky. Quick introductions, a brief stop in the kitchen to fix a couple of nightcaps and then off to your room. Remember, you are a grown woman and you needn't do any sort of giggling, sheepish routine with your flatmates.

A word of caution here: keep in mind what the alcohol intake was during the evening. Have you already shared a bottle of wine and had two snifters of brandy each? Then make those drinks little ones. You might also bring your guest a glass of water, whether he asks for it or not. Without drawing his attention to your concern, you don't want him consuming too much more alcohol unless your idea of fun is a conversation about how 'this' has never happened to him before. If very few drinks have been had, then go ahead and pour each of you a big whisky. Too much alcohol is only slightly worse than not enough prior to getting naked with someone for the first time.

Don't worry about making the first move. Of course if you want to, that's great. He will surely be glad you did. If you're more in the mood to be seduced, then proceed as follows. Until you are ready, keep the conversation moving. Then just stop talking and look at him and smile a little. This always works.

DRESSING AND UNDRESSING

Even an FG can feel apprehensive at the thought of being naked with a new partner. This is quite natural, which is why natural lighting is the best way to set the tone and create FG ambience. If you live alone, then all you must worry about now is setting the scene. Wherever you may be, light a few candles (or at least dim the lights), put on some quiet music and pour a couple of drinks. One candle will give off enough light so that skin will look great but not too detailed. The best option is, of course, moonlight, but since that isn't always possible, street lighting can illuminate your bedroom quite well. In fact, it is highly recommended that you study your room at different times of day to learn when is the best time for the desired effect.

For a planned first night with a new boy, an FG should:

- wear her obligatory matching bra and underwear or none at all;
- clean her room and change her sheets (extra throw pillows add a harem-tent look);
- open blinds or curtains to let in natural or street light;
- have a candle and matches within striking distance;
- have condoms in the bedside cabinet drawer;
- have a dressing gown or nightie a fingertip away;
- have breath-freshening mints to hand.

For an impromptu first night with a new boy an FG should refrain from saying 'my place is such a mess'; simply pour him a drink, excuse yourself and run to your bedroom for a quick tidy-up and to change into your sexy underwear (though a true FG will always have them on).

An FG should expect the same sort of treatment when she is at his place for the first time, though it is highly recommended that you retire to your own home as often as possible since all of your skin and hair products are there. But if you do end up in his pad, then you may ask him if you can light some candles or open the blinds and turn off the halogen floor lamp that lights up the whole block. He may not have thought of it. If you're a modest FG, then after sex you may 'shiver' and ask to borrow a T-shirt because you are often 'cold' at night. You will then have something for cover in the morning.

FIRST-NIGHT OBLIGATIONS

During the first night in bed, there are a few things that must occur. Of course, every Fabulous Girl is hoping for world-rocking orgasms – not to mention the possibility that the new lover suddenly morphs into Hugh Grant (sigh) – during that first encounter. Alas, it is more often the case that neither eventuality presents itself. Nervousness, unfamiliarity and the predictable effects of one-too-many glasses of red wine may have their way with you more than he can. Nevertheless, an effort should be made by both partners. It's only polite.

Just as you wouldn't dream of meeting someone without saying hello, so too should you in the bedroom introduction. That's right, we mean oral sex, so get down there and say a quick but friendly hello to everyone involved. It needn't be a lengthy discourse, just 'Hi, it's wonderful to meet you'. And you absolutely should expect a reciprocal greeting from the new lover. Not only does the absence of this nicety reflect a lack of manners on his part, it may bode poorly for your sexual future with him.

THE MORNING AFTER

Great sex or not, a polite 'good morning' chat is in order. You needn't allude to the act itself; it may be wiser not to in case your 'that was amazing' is not returned. Depending on the length of your acquaintance (fifth date, friends for years and then boom or one-night stand), you may feel snuggly but keep to the generalities of 'What's your plan for the day?'

This gives both of you an out if the last thing you want is to spend the day together.

No matter what your intentions are, get dressed in the morning. Strolling around nude (or even in pyjamas) is intimate, couple behaviour. Yeah, it's true that you got more than naked with him last night. But just so that no-one mistakes sex for love, get dressed. Besides, people can look 'different' the next morning, and sometimes sobriety and daylight make for unpleasant discoveries. It's especially nice to offer that spare dressing gown you keep on hand or a clean T-shirt. Just be aware that you may not ever see the garment again.

Be gallant and offer him first dibs on the shower (in case he wants to take flight asap). Share your toothbrush. It's very rude to be squeamish about toothbrushes with someone you've slept with. And it's better than showing off your extensive collection of brand-new ones kept for this purpose.

How you both handle breakfast tells you as much about what's going on between you as the night before. If the sleep-over occurred at your place, you really should offer him something no matter how you feel. You fucked him, you can pour him a glass of orange juice. That's all you have to do if you're feeling mortified. Even if you don't think he's boyfriend material, you can still give him a bowl of cornflakes and a coffee. Reserve the offer to make smoked salmon and scrambled eggs or, best of all, an invitation to the greasy spoon around the corner for a guy you really like. (Is there anything more romantic than a greasy spoon on a Sunday at noon? All those sex-drunk, messy-haired new couples sharing the Sunday papers?) This is vital. There's something about a special breakfast on weekend mornings that makes people want to go back to bed and have sex again: use them with caution.

If you stayed at his, you'll know exactly how he feels about you based on the kind of breakfast offer you receive. See above.

If sex preceded courtship, then you can definitely ask for his number the next morning. Or you can offer yours and see if he reciprocates. Better than playing the number game, though, is to make a specific invitation: 'I'm going to the Tracey Emin opening next Thursday, are you interested?' You have to be prepared for a let-down. If this is too perilous for you, you need to rethink casual sex. If you are one without thoughts of a repeat performance, be clear – nicely – right now. And go ahead and lie: 'I'm not ready to date yet. I guess I'm still not over Bingo yet' is better than 'I really needed to get laid last night'.

Even Fabulous Girls have sex for wrong or confused reasons sometimes. And it's perfectly normal to feel lonely and bad after a one-night stand if it was affection you were really after. It's not all right, though, to be bitter and pissed off with the guy you slept with. If you didn't know your own motivations, how could he? What you should definitely expect is kindness and friendliness post-casual sex. Unfortunately, many men get terrified and assume that you'll want to be choosing china patterns if he so much as gets acquainted with your breasts. All an FG can do is to know her own mind about sex and hope that her relaxed attitude will put the new lover at ease.

THE MIDNIGHT RUN

If one of you decides that post-coital cuddling is not on the cards, can you bid adieu without being rude? An FG may flee if she has a dog to walk or has to go to work the next day and her stiletto heels and bustier won't go down well at the 8 a.m. board meeting. You should indicate this before you have sex. If the sex was so awful that you can't stomach him touching you another second, then a polite but crisp 'I can't stay' or 'I never sleep over the first night; it's a rule I have' will suffice. In fact, many men will be relieved.

If it is your boy Bingo who wants to run, let him. Likewise, he should make bolting excuses earlier in the evening. If not, then it is a sign that he really wants out of there. This type of behaviour is truly one-night-stand stuff.

THE CALL

The hours that pass between when you first have sex with a new lover and when the telephone rings tell you a great deal about what will take place in the future. Let's say you and the lucky guy did it on Saturday night. And let's say it was probably about 2 a.m. when you finally got around to it. An FG expects the first call to come in no later than thirty-six hours after sex.

Scenario 1. He calls Sunday night, after dinner = he's keen on you and definitely wants to start something up.

Scenario 2. He calls by 2 p.m. Monday afternoon = he wants to sleep with you again, or at least keep his options open.

Scenario 3. He calls Sunday afternoon as soon as he gets home = he's desperate. It's too soon to call, and this behaviour should be discouraged. Everyone needs a little space after the first night.

Scenario 4. He calls on Wednesday, any time of day = he's not really interested at all but is starting to think about next weekend.

Scenario 5. He calls on Friday night at about 11.30 = he wants to come over. For sex. That's it.

An FG can certainly make any of these calls herself. If you had a nice time, particularly if you had a nice time at his place, it's polite and friendly to call and let him know. It doesn't have to be a big deal. 'Just wanted to say thanks for having me'.

SOUVENIRS

Like a notch in a belt, some women choose to collect items from lovers as tokens of their night together. Whether it's sweatshirts or lighters, this is not a practice of an FG – at least not after you've left school.

Admitting Important Facts

As an FG grows older, there are certain things that may have happened to her that she should disclose to a potential mate. The same rules apply to the gentleman, of course. When is the appropriate time to confess a previous marriage, impending divorce, children or the like? Of course children are difficult to hide, and an FG is better off disclosing this information before the date takes place, say, during a phone conversation or an e-mail. It may seem tempting to wait until the man's interest is secured, but it is really an ill-mannered trick. You also risk getting hurt because you allowed yourself to get emotionally involved during this deceit and he may walk the second he learns of it. The Fabulous Girl is not a game player; she prides herself on her honesty and forthrightness. An FG will tell the bloke straight off about the kid (or kids) and then stand firm while he runs either away from or towards her.

Impending divorces and previous marriages can be held back until you are more sure of your feelings. Quite frankly, the fact that an FG was once married is no-one's business but her own. If it becomes clear that she will continue to see said man, then she can tell him. There is something infinitely sexy about a divorcee.

If, however, your date confesses that he is still married, then it is a major slight to you, not to mention the major slight it is to his wife. The old adage 'What kind of a girl do you think I am?' is not out of place here. Any reaction from a drink in his face to storming out of the restaurant to ordering the most expensive thing on the menu with a calm façade will do.

SEXUAL HISTORY

All the talk concerning sexual health and the risk of STDs might have you believing that probing your new beau's past is strictly an issue of safety. And of course, a girl can't be too careful when it comes to her health. No matter what a man tells you about his sexual past, a modern woman takes responsibility for her own health and acts as if he's been up to more than he's confessing to – which is almost certainly true.

There are, of course, polite ways to uncover sexual history. The FG should feel confident bringing up sex at dinner on the intended first night; it's far enough from the actual event so as not to ruin the mood, and he'll be so distracted by his second favourite thing in life – food – that he won't recognize your strategy. A few straightforward questions or personal revelations will get the job done: 'I donated blood for the first time last week. Have you ever done that?' or 'Do you have a long list of exes?' Questions asked in a flirty but matter-of-fact manner will elicit honest responses. It is then up to you to decide if he's for you.

Any way you slice it, condoms are a must. They're also no big deal. Tolerate no whinging when it comes to their deployment. And Fabulous Girls will appreciate the tidiness of the easy-to-dispose-of package.

But let's face it, you're not curious about his past only because you're worried about the clap. You want to know about the other women: what he liked, what he's done, what turned him off. And if you've been sleeping together for more than a couple of weeks, it's perfectly acceptable pillow talk to do a little prying – as long as you're willing to reciprocate, naturally. Questions like 'Where's the weirdest place you've done it?' or 'How old were you when you first tried that?' are not a problem, and his answers will tell you a lot about your sexual future with him. Asking about kinky girlfriends of old is a sly way of finding out whether your new lover is a prude (and maybe that's fine with you) or a full-on sexual adventurer (and maybe that's fine with you, too).

If you're serious about each other, you should avoid questions about the most recent girlfriend. At least for several months, you shouldn't talk about her in a sexual context. Men are protective of the women they love (or loved), and if he still harbours feelings for her, it will get his back up. And it's not good for you, either, to picture someone else so recently with him.

This is a game of tit-for-tat. Stories must be told in equal measure. Start with easy confessions ('My first time was a ridiculous disaster') before coughing up anything too wild ('I did it with my cousin one summer').

Sex, Sex, Sex

HOW TO GET WHAT YOU WANT IN THE BEDROOM

You can be the best lover any man has ever had. Enjoy sex. Let him know that you enjoy sex, especially with him. Be enthusiastic and lusty about his body. We realize it is the knee-jerk reaction of most FGs to simply expect physical adoration. That's just fine. But sex is a situation where showing up is not 90 per cent. Showing up is 50per cent and effort is the rest.

Of course there is such a thing as chemistry, and some people only have to make eye contact to know they're going to have great sex together. But when things aren't going so swimmingly, you needn't despair. You can create your own best lover in him – mostly. Just react to a man as if he were brilliant in bed and watch him improve. Praising him for doing the things you like – even if he's never, ever touched the spot behind your knee that drives you crazy – will ensure that he'll start a career of knee-pit touching. Remember, men like to be good at things, so it's always better to offer praise than criticism.

While no-one can make you do anything you don't want to, when it comes to sex, an FG should try to be as flexible and open-minded as she can. A little generosity goes a long way. If he's mustered up the courage to tell you he's got a thing for white cotton knickers, don't flip out and start dialling Childline; get over yourself and pick up a three-pack at M&S. No-one's asking you to break any of your moral codes, so unless it's something that truly makes your skin crawl, give it a try. When you're in a relationship, you have to start thinking about sex in the long term. Not every time has to be about you. Nonetheless, going outside of your own comfort zone with sex does involve an emotional risk, so it's wise to wait until you feel good in a relationship before you start any really wild experimentation.

REQUESTS FROM THE FRINGE

The top ten requests from men are:

1. Telling and hearing fantasies. If this is hard for you, you need to talk to your shrink about it.

2. Talking dirty while having sex. Also an easy one. Just do it.

3. Watching porn. The only real problem here is that most porn is so astonishingly bad. And FGs, with their heightened aesthetic sensibilities, may find the bad acting and nasty lighting more than they can bear. Go to a woman-friendly sex shop and ask for help finding something that can do it for both of you.

4. Making porn together. Just remember: videotape is for ever.

5. Stripping. Why not put on a show at home?

6. Shaving. If you agree to go pre-pubescent for him, have it waxed professionally rather than let him lather you up. One false move with a razor down there and things could get ugly.

7. Bondage. Occasionally you'll come across a man who still thinks tying you up to the bed is the naughtiest thing anyone has ever imagined. Go ahead and make his day. No-one ever ties those flimsy silk scarves tight enough to really restrain you anyway, so what the hell?

8. Multiple partners. He always wants to do it with you and another woman, so stop waiting for the day that he suggests bringing his cute friend Bruce to bed with you both. Don't try this with friends. If you think you can handle group sex, best not to introduce jealousy into the mix by watching your man do it with Sally from your Pilates class.

9. Public spaces. There are reasons that Fabulous Girls occasionally wear skirts and dresses sans underwear. But skip the communal jacuzzi.

10. Anal sex. It's really up to you, but no-one has the right to expect it. And if that's all he's interested in, you may have a problem.

Of course the Fabulous Girl is free to explore her own desires and in fact will appear all the more sexually free and wild if she initiates the fantasy or special request. While an FG loves being seduced (it goes well with the need to be adored), she is also expert in the art of seduction. Initiating sex should be sophisticated and polite. Nothing is more unsexy than 'So do you want to do it?'

SEXUAL CONUNDRUMS

Couples have the luxury of time to work out their sexual differences and quirks and the minor embarrassments that come with an intimate relationship. But even if you're a sexy single whose sex life is more of the fling variety, there's no reason not to apply good manners to sticky situations. Here are the rules of decorum for gracious negotiation of sexual awkwardness:

1. 'This has never happened to me before'. Nerves and the late-night-and-lots-of-drinks combo that usually describe the casual-sex scenario can create unfortunate disabilities, even in the most virile. As the lover, you must of course be as kind as possible but also not spend too much time on the topic. Why not make a virtue of it and get creative? And both parties should relax and remember that morning-after sex can be well worth waiting for.

2. 'Did you?' Much like the above. Jitters can stop many women from experiencing an earth-shattering conclusion with a new lover. It does not mean she didn't have a good time. No faking it. You don't want to reinforce bad moves. So go ahead and admit it. He'll appreciate the challenge.

3. 'Would you mind...?' It's never rude to turn down requests from the sexual fringe made by a casual lover. If you happen to love the idea of dressing up like a nurse and administering the special prescription, then consider it your lucky day when your new man suggests just that scenario. In a long-term relationship, it's necessary to be flexible to allow for your partner's sexual happiness, but a fling just doesn't

demand the same kind of consideration. A polite 'No, I don't think so' is fine.

4. 'Uh-oh.' The condom broke. You may have only just met, but you are both now in a dilemma together. Sorry, but this is a case of paying the piper. If you want to head immediately for the doctor or chemist to get a morning-after pill, then he's got to go too. You should expect a call the next day to see how you're feeling (which will be terrible because those pills are nasty).

HOW MUCH SEX

There is a very definite connection between the soundness of your relationship and the amount of sex you have. People who deny this aren't having a lot of sex. If you are having sex once a day (or more), you are in a new relationship. This is a great period in your life, but sooner or later you'll have to go to work and meet your girlfriends for coffee. If you're living together and having sex three times a week or more, you are in a happy, healthy relationship. If things have slowed down to once a week, someone isn't happy about it. Either you or he doesn't like the way things have cooled down and is wondering why. You've probably had a couple of really fun conversations about it too. If you're not having sex even once a week, your relationship is officially on the rocks. If one of you doesn't want sex more than this, then you are living with a flatmate, not a lover. The time may come when you look at your man and realize he repulses you – you can't stand the thought of him touching you. You cannot tell him this. But you must break up (see the chapter on couples).

Dating Variations

CHEATERS NEVER PROSPER –
UNLESS THEY FOLLOW THE INFIDELITY COMMANDMENTS

It is not uncommon for an FG to be attracted to a married man. In fact, at a certain point in her life, she may be really interested in married men. If, for example, she does not wish for commitment but only for sex, then the married man is perfect. Or if she's over thirty and single, she may discover that most men are married and that some of them either lie about it or want to have an affair. The moral choice is up to her, but the chances are it will not end well.

We aren't advocating extramarital activities, but if you must, do it our way: politely. Herewith are the Ten Commandments of Infidelity:

- Thou shalt use protection, so as not to spread nasty diseases to any spouses or face awkward paternity questions.
- Thou shalt make up viable excuses for your newly acquired tardiness so that your spouse can pretend to believe you. Practise lying in front of the mirror.
- Thou shalt perform illicit acts only outside of the marital bed. Anyway, adultery makes one hungry, so the two of you can partake of room service in the more appropriate setting of a hotel.
- Thou shalt never hint at leaving your spouse as a method of maintaining your side dish's interest.
- Thou shalt begin saving up for a divorce trust fund.
- Thou shalt not call during dinner or at any other time you know your lover is devoting 'quality' time to family.
- Thou shalt not try to become your lover's spouse's friend. If you already are, then pull away. Slowly.
- Thou shalt not confess – that is, brag about – your sins to anyone. Except, of course, to your very best friend, whom

you must expect to tell his or her significant other. But it stops there. Need to get it off your chest? Get a therapist. Anything more is selfish and definitely not polite.

- Thou shalt not pry into the details of your lover's marriage, especially not the sex – after all, you're not after a ménage-à-trois, are you? – or offer up the dirt on your husband's sexual prowess or lack thereof.
- Thou shalt not keep asking your lover when he is going to leave the marriage. It's not going to happen. (And if it does, you may regret it.) Thou shalt not promise to leave your own.
- Thou shalt not drink and dial. (We know this makes eleven commandments, but this last one cannot be over-stated.)

DATING WHILE DATING

It used to be that when you were out with Bingo – even for the first time – you only had eyes for him. At least, you had to pretend you did. Now, if Bingo is boring or if commitment is not yet on the table, there needn't be the pretence that you're taken. So you're on your way to powder your nose and you bump into foxy filmmaker Felix. Sparks fly. If he asks for your number, you can in good conscience slip your card in his pocket. But that's it for now. If you're out on a date with Bingo, you mustn't ask Felix out. You can always hunt him down tomorrow. And if you know he's asking you out while on a date with Fifi – the rogue! – he must be taught a lesson. Decline his request. Above all, discretion, please. There's no need to hurt Bingo's feelings. And if you're planning on using Felix's interest as a tool for inflaming Bingo's passions, forget it. It never works.

VIRTUAL DATING

Many people meet members of the opposite sex over the Internet, whether in chat rooms or in the classifieds. This doesn't have the same negative reputation that traditional personal ads or dating services do. Many young, vibrant people are exploring the Web, and because of its ease and distance (with no voice or face-to-face encounter), they are taking the chance to find someone to their liking.

There are, however, certain protocols to respect.

Photos
Exchange a picture asap. It must be a recent photo, no more than two years old. This will eliminate many from your roster of prospective beaux. Never kid yourself that getting to know someone only by e-mail will mean that you will fall in love and it won't matter what he looks like. Looks matter.

When to talk on the phone
With so many people owning mobiles, voice-to-voice communication is less of an invasion of space. After you've seen a person's recent photo, e-mailed past histories and established common interests, then you may wish to proceed to the second level of communication. He should be more willing to give his number than you. In fact, it is wise to only share your mobile; never your home number. As sexist as this sounds, the majority of stalking and violence is perpetrated by men. He should respect your concern for your safety. The phone call itself may not go well the first time. You will both be nervous. If you like his voice and he does engage you in conversation, this may tell you that he'll be diverting in person.

When to meet face to face

Phase three of the virtual world is reality world. As on any blind or personal-ad date, meet in a public place, arrange your own transportation and leave his name and number and where you're meeting him with a close friend. If, however, you meet him and are not interested (and it takes mere seconds to determine your attraction), you do not have to remain out with him longer than one hour. One drink will do. You also do not need to tell him then and there if you want to see him again. If he asks directly, tell him 'friends first' or better, e-mail him.

ROMANTIC E-MAIL ETIQUETTE

1. Making casual social plans. All socializing is fine on e-mail. If someone's account is through their office, though, take are with the content of your messages. Messages can be accessed by IT, accidentally be printed and cause embarrassment for all.

2. Romantic letters are all the more romantic if hand-written, and more memorable too. However, they may be sent using e-mail; in fact, the Internet has sped up the love-selection process. Be wary of workplace e-mails for privacy's sake, but a sweetly worded letter popping up in one's inbox can perk up anyone's day.

3. Never cancel a date by e-mail. Just make the phone call.

4. Never end a relationship by e-mail, unless it is solely an Internet romance. Where once the 'Dear John' letter reigned, followed by the 'Let's be friends' phone call, the e-mail break-up has taken over, becoming the rudest and most cowardly of them all.

DATING A FAMOUS PERSON

Not every Fabulous Girl will have the opportunity to date a famous person. If, however, those are the circles in which you run, then there must be certain rules of propriety. First, remember that it's your affair; keep it to yourself. Telling your mother or best friend is permissible; telling the check-out girl at Joseph is not. In fact, your celebrity beau will expect you to be discreet or you can kiss him goodbye. It is a clever FG who maintains an aura of secrecy around her movie-star man. Your discretion will provide your friends with hours of great gossip and speculation.

One downside to celebrity is the fans. When out with him, you will have to endure countless pretty young things groping him and interrupting fine dinners – or worse, you will be shoved out of the way by autograph hounds. Smile and keep telling yourself that he's going home with you.

His people, managers, agents and PR reps will get to know you, and you must befriend them. They will prove to be invaluable in granting you access to your man.

The other downside of courting the famous is that the FG will be second banana – not an easy thing for her. If he's the right sort of man, he will hold her hand in public and introduce her to other industry types, always making her feel valued. If he does not, then he is a cad and you may need to move on.

CADS AND VILLAINS

There are countless boyfriends to wade through before an FG finds the man whose appreciation of style, luxury, wit and intellect matches her own. She will date one or more less-than-desirable males – it is an unavoidable rite of passage. However, she may try to recognize them before she decides to embark on the commitment trail.

Herewith is the Fabulous Girl's list of Cads and Villains, with descriptions, dangers and early warning signs:

The Dark Brooder

An FG can naturally be fooled by assuming that this man's silence masks a deep thinker. He may not be writing the next great novel in his head. He may just be a simpleton. There is something inherently sexy in the loner, the rebel and the angry young man. Though he can exist at any age, this boy is better got over with at school.

Danger Zone: An FG feels that only she can unlock the mystery of this man's hidden personality. She wants to be his confidante, to bring to light his simmering talent, to protect him from those who don't understand him. What really happens is that she listens to all his ramblings, but if she presses him to open up, he shuts her down, stammering that no-one understands him and he needs to be alone. Then he comes back for sex.

Early Warning Signs: Has few friends. Does not socialize much, preferring to sip Scotch on his sofa and watch the Weather Channel. Hardly says a word on your first few dates but surprises you when he keeps calling and inviting you over for sex. No work of art or writing ever materializes. He will tell you his dreams but he never lifts a finger to further his ambitions.

The Musician

Few FGs can resist the temptation of a guy on stage swinging his hips, singing just for her. That big guitar of his just can't be turned down. It's even more of an attraction if you love his music and his stage clothes.

Danger Zone: The FG immediately wants him all to herself and needs to distinguish herself from the groupies.

Early Warning Signs: He's a musician.

175

The Player

This Casanova, not to be confused with the Chronic Cheat (read on), actually loves women. He loves their company, their minds and their attitudes as well as their breasts and long legs. He is attracted to all sorts of body types. Unfortunately, the world has so many to choose from that he finds it difficult to stay true to one girl.

Danger Zone: He is a great listener who makes the FG feel gorgeous, sexy and appreciated. He's a great lover. But for an FG who wants a relationship, he is too randy. He is the perfect sort for a fling. An FG needs to decide what she wants before entering into the sultan's tent with this one.

Early Warning Signs: He has a large female following of friends and admirers, many of whom are ex-lovers; they embrace and kiss him at all his favourite haunts. He tells you he has never been in a relationship longer than six months. He has only limited amounts of time to see you and has little interest in meeting your friends (especially couples or Chapsticks) and relatives.

The Chronic Cheat

This scoundrel is a villain of the first order and doesn't like or trust women. He thinks of his girlfriend as a trophy or as easy sex. His repeated philandering is guilt-free, and he never thinks he'll get caught. He does not believe in monogamy but will not openly admit this because he is too immature for a real discussion. Of course he could not cope if his girlfriend ever cheated on him.

Danger Zone: Ignorance is bliss. An FG may even know of his habitual cheating but feel that he will behave differently with her. She will try to change her look for him, to be everything he wants, which is impossible because what he wants is another girl – all the time.

Early Warning Signs: He repeatedly says, 'Sex is just sex, it has nothing to do with love'.

The One-Sided Man

He never calls when he says he will or when etiquette demands he should (e.g. the day after sex). He never suggests getting together but agrees to go out when the woman asks. Any time she wants to speak to him, she's the one picking up the phone. Welcome to the one-sided relationship. This guy is no gentleman. He will only see her when it is convenient and he has little regard for her time or feelings.

Danger Zone: This rogue confuses the FG, for although he never pursues her actively, he is most attentive when he is with her. Thus she convinces herself that he's simply Mr Busy-Guy and does the chasing on her own. This can be a novelty but will grow dull in a short time.

Early Warning Signs: He never calls unless returning your call. He makes little effort to communicate or spend time with you unless initiated by you. He seems not to notice that it's been two weeks since you last spoke with him.

The Too-Nice Guy

This particular man tries to fix everything. He feels that to solve all your problems will make you love him. And worse, he never disagrees with you.

Danger Zone: This is often the rebound man. After an FG breaks it off with, say, the Dark Brooder, she will find comfort in a Too-Nice Guy. Unfortunately, too many Too-Nice Guys try too hard, and this proves their undoing. It simply grates on an FG's nerves.

Early Warning Signs: He buys you stuffed animals, flowers and chocolate for no reason, all the time.

The Walking Wounded

Permanently scarred by bad parents or evil ex-girlfriends, this man cannot move forward. He not only blames all his woes on others from his past, he wallows in his misery.

Danger Zone: An FG feels that she can save him, teach him what love really is and keep him happy for ever. This is wrong. He is only happy when he is miserable, and he will drag an FG through such mires of unhealthy depression that she is wise to avoid him.

Early Warning Signs: On the first date, he divulges too much personal information about his abusive parents, their divorce and how he hasn't got over it. He calls his ex awful names.

The Toy Boy

Neither a cad nor a villain, this boy is younger than the FG, usually under thirty. He is virile and sexy and he adores her. He may, however, not be mature enough for a lasting relationship and will at some point need to go off and find himself.

Danger Zone: The FG doesn't go in with her eyes open and tries to convince herself and all her friends that he's really mature for his age.

Early Warning Signs: He repeatedly requires lengthy conversations and advice about his goals and how he might achieve them. He has no goals.

THE SIGNS

With any man, you will know from the first day if he's going to be right for you – maybe not for ever, but at least with real potential. An FG knows herself, but that knowledge is easy to forget if the man is cute or if she is lonely or insecure when she meets him. And it happens to all FGs. The guy will say or do something that really irritates her or goes against a strong grain of hers, but she will overlook that fault because, well, he likes her. And if he likes her, she must like him, right? She will make excuses, talk herself out of his hatred of dogs, convince herself that he's just nervous around them and once he meets Rex it will be love. Watch for the early signs; those little things that irritate you on the first date or two will come back to haunt you. An FG should never be afraid to walk away when her intuition is telling her he's wrong. Patience and intuition are her best weapon against bad relationships.

HAPPINESS RADAR

He's the one that demolished you. You knew in the very depth of your subconscious that it would never work out, but you held on six months longer than anyone thought was reasonable. And then he dumped you. It took you a year to get over it. Slowly, you have pulled yourself together and actually started checking out guys again.

And that's when the call comes. There's that guy who dumped you, who will always sense when you're about to get over him and get on with your life. This kind of telepathy has been known to work even from great distances. If you're not careful, it's possible to be set back by such a call, particularly if it comes with the typical 'Can I come over?' at the end. Of course, it's very tempting to want to hook up with the one who ditched you. It proves, in some demented way, that he was wrong and that you really are desirable. But know that you will probably only hear from this kind of man when you are just about to move further away from him.

THE NICE GUY

By the time you are twenty-five, you must make it a top priority to do away with all the sexy scumbags that seemed so irresistible in your early twenties. You must also do something that seems at once perfectly obvious and revolutionary:

start finding nice men attractive. If you've had a long career of falling for bad guys, this will take some work. Don't fall for the ridiculous notion that Nice Guys are boring. Or that the sex will be dull. Rather, think that a queen such as yourself deserves to be treated with respect and affection. Once you add Nice Guys to the list of possible mates, the floodgates truly open. There are in fact a great many nice men out there who are being ignored by women (you only have to bring up this topic among nice men to hear them rage about the way women seem to prefer bad guys to them).

I wondered if there would be a message from G.G. on my machine when I got home. It had been two weeks since our encounter on the street. Maybe filming had started? Maybe it was a night shoot? Maybe he thought I was covered in scales?

At three weeks, I started to get annoyed about the whole thing. There was no reason I couldn't call him. I phoned the local independent filmmakers' association to get his number. He obviously liked me, and there's nothing wrong with calling a guy you like. That I spent a week considering what I'd say was embarrassing but also, I think, a learning experience about what men go through regularly on this issue.

I phoned in the morning, hoping he'd be at work so I could just leave a message. I practised in my head. Breezy, upbeat.

'Hello.'

'Oh, you're home,' I said.

'Yes, who is this?'

'Oh, God, right. Sorry it's me. Spilling Scotch. Slipping business cards into men's pockets.' I laughed and wished I hadn't.

'Hey, how are you?'

'I'm fine. How's the film going?'

'Postponed. Next month for sure – unless it's not. You know.'

'I'm sorry to hear that. I'm sure it'll work out.' What was I saying? What I knew about how it would work out was nothing. I pushed on. 'I'm calling, actually, to see if you wanted to go out for a drink some time. Whenever.'

'Um, well, aren't you and that guy...?'

'Felix? Oh, no. I mean, we were, uh, that was just a thing. He's not my boyfriend, wasn't my boyfriend. We were just hanging out and I'm not doing...that any more.' I wanted to hang up. Even more, I wanted to hit my own head as hard as I could with the receiver.

'I see,' he laughed. 'A thing. Well, if you're not having a thing with anyone, then I'd love to have a drink.'

I had to hand it to myself: for a shy girl, I was doing very well, but I was ready for him to start being the boy and suggest a time and a place. He, however, wasn't going for that plan. I only had to suggest two times and one location before we could set a date, and it wasn't more painful than having my teeth drilled, I guess. And it left me with three days to worry about what I was going to wear.

I took Eleanor's advice and went for what she calls 'accidentally cute'. The key to accidental cuteness is that at least one element of the outfit must be casual. You definitely do not want to appear like you took the time you actually did to get ready. So here's what I wore: a flowery (but not too girlie), chiffon slip dress that's cut low enough to give even me a bit of cleavage, flat sandals and a denim jacket. Hair and make-up not obvious. The littlest bit of perfume.

Sitting at the bar, I was feeling pretty good. A couple of guys checked me out while they walked through to the restaurant beyond the bar, but in a polite, subtle way. I ordered a vodka tonic. I don't care what anyone says, I *can* taste the difference between Stoli and Absolut, and Stoli is better. I finished it even though I was taking the smallest sips I could to slow down what was becoming a tortuous wait. I started to doubt myself. Had we said 8.30? Had I said it was on College Street? It was getting to be very hard to maintain the relaxed pose I'd struck at the bar. Of course, the waiters could see exactly what was happening. Why else the sympathetic smiles? Finally, Daniel gestured me over to the phone.

'Hello?'

'It's me, I'm so sorry I'm not there.'

'I'd sort of noticed.'

'There was a crisis in my family today and I had to take my brother to the hospital.'

'Is everything OK?'

'It turns out to be nothing really. Still, I think I'd better hang out here with him for a while. I'm really sorry I didn't catch you earlier. Do you mind if we make it another night?'

'No, of course not. Sure, let's do it another night.' There was a pause. Daniel wanted me to get off the phone so he could put a Visa through.

'I'd love to see you tomorrow if you're free,' he said.

'I think that's fine. Same time and place?'

'Great. Thanks for being so sweet about this.'

'Oh, it's nothing.'

The family crisis did not come up the next night. After a couple of drinks on the busy café-studded street, we jumped in a cab to go to a rooftop bar in town. Except that once we got in the cab, we started pawing each other as if that was the plan we'd made for the night. *Three glasses of red then I'm going to put my tongue in your mouth in the back seat of a taxi, OK?* G.G. gave the cabbie his address and we went there instead.

He had his own flat in the leafy neighbourhood surrounding the university. That was a first for me, a guy without flatmates (if you don't count that other guy's wife). It's a whole new ball game having sex with someone who lives alone. You can do it on the couch. You can do it on the kitchen table. You can do it on the stairs up to his room. And of course, you can do it on his big bed. And so we did.

'I'll talk to you soon,' he said as he smooched me one last time on his doorstep. The walk of shame didn't feel shameful in the least as I strolled through the leafy streets on my way home.

So that was on a Friday, and I called him on Sunday night. I tried to resist. Not calling on Saturday was an amazing feat of self-restraint. My stomach flipped with every ring of the phone. My mum. Missy. Eleanor. Every phone call but the one I wanted. Finally at 9 p.m. on Sunday, I had to do it.

'Hello?' Classical music playing in the background.

'Hi, it's me.'

'Hi, it's so nice to hear your voice.'

'Yeah?'

'How are you? What did you do all weekend?'

'Oh, very busy,' I said, sticking my tongue out at myself in the hallway mirror. 'I went out to a party last night. It was a laugh. Were you around?'

'Yeah, I did some work at home, basically nothing. You should have called me,' he said.

'Well, I wasn't sure...you know.'

'What do you mean?'

'Well, I don't know, do you want to come over now? *The Third Man* is on TV tonight.'

'Sure, give me your address again.'

In my experience, seeing a new guy who you think you

could really like twice in one weekend is a sure sign of escalating romance. And that feeling that you're both eager to see each other again as soon as possible can be intoxicating. But if you're the one who is initiating all the arrangements, it can appear like it's heating up – a trompe l'oeil of romance, if you will – when you're the only one going up.

Couples

There we all were, about to partake in our first dinner party in coupledom. We were at Eleanor's. I had Groovy Guy and I was smitten. Bingo was back and Eleanor and he were all snuggly – much to the disgust of Missy and me. Then of course there was Missy. Still single. Still sarcastic. 'Did you hear about that recent study that showed that married women are more likely to suffer from severe depression and suicidal tendencies than single girls?'

Eleanor had gone to the fuss of making beef Wellington, and we were ready to feast. We had all lifted our glasses in a toast to the chef, when the annoying ring of a mobile phone shook the moment. And worse, it wasn't a normal ring-ring, but one of those childish sing-song rings whose muzak melody goes on for eternity; and worse than that, it belonged to Groovy Guy; and even worse, he answered it as if it was the most natural thing to do in the world. Our tableau remained frozen for what seemed like minutes while we all waited in disbelief for Groovy Guy to quickly hang up and apologize. It didn't happen. So I did the sensible thing and kicked him under the table. Startled, he looked up and, I thought, read the horror on my face.

'Just hold on a second,' he snapped to the caller. Relief flooded my face. 'Cheers!' Groovy Guy announced, clinking his glass to no-one in particular and gulping his wine. Then he stood up and walked outside to the balcony, the sliding glass door thudding us out from his top-secret call.

'I'm sure it's a very important conversation,' offered Missy, though I thought I detected a satisfied smirk. Eleanor nodded. Bingo, who was barely present anyway, poked at his plate and said dimly, 'I don't like meat and pastry together. It's unnatural.' He left the table to investigate other culinary possibilities. Eleanor shot back her glass of wine. I wanted to shoot both Bingo and Groovy Guy. Missy shot us a look of single contentment and sipped her Merlot.

I forgave – or rather I overlooked – Groovy Guy's blunders in manners in exchange for the emotional stability I craved. After all, I had a career and a great flat and I needed the great guy to complete the picture. I wanted to singlehandedly disprove Eleanor's theory that a girl can't have all three at the same time. Still it surprised me when after only five months, Groovy Guy brought up the subject of moving in together. After the one-sided nature of our courtship, I felt convinced that I would be the first one to broach the subject of cohabitation. Of course there was no doubt that (a) I would say yes and (b) he would move into my place. But it still shocked me on moving day when my gorgeous apartment was suddenly flooded with big, black audiovisual equipment, golf clubs and ugly '70s leftover furniture from his mother. I had seen all this stuff before, obviously, but I had never thought about it actually being in my flat, er, our place.

The first few weeks were bliss. I managed to find ample storage space so that Groovy's belongings were safe and out of sight. We cooked together, watched videos and cocooned. We even bought a kitten. We named her Kitty, our cute, red ball of fluff. I loved her. Groovy tolerated her.

Couples

The mistake many people make when it comes to manners is in thinking that the better you know someone, the less necessary good manners become. Nothing could be further from the truth. If manners are a sign of respect and care for others, then etiquette should flourish in a relationship.

It's vital to a healthy relationship to keep having sex. But it's just as important to keep saying 'please' and 'thank you'. In fact, there is something strangely sexy about retaining a strain of formality between partners. Behaving in a polite way towards your partner reminds both of you that you don't take each other for granted.

ARE YOU MY BOYFRIEND?

If you have been dating for a length of time, you will eventually have to have the conversation and use the *c* word. The polite *c* word: *commitment*. Add *relationship* to the dialogue and you will be able to determine where you stand. There is a large divide between 'seeing someone' and 'I have a boyfriend'. If you are not anxious for a boyfriend, you can avoid this conversation; he probably will. If, however, you find that your feelings are growing for him, then it is not impolite to ask, 'Are we becoming exclusive?' Obviously if you are spending every night in each other's arms and going out in public holding hands, such a question won't be necessary. This is the type of relationship an FG aspires to. Welcome to the land of the couple.

The Real Rules

When the Fabulous Girl is single, she is carefree and does what she wants to when she wants to do it. This is also true for single men. A new set of etiquette rules will help couples adjust to the demands of their new life together.

CALLING

Call when you say you will call. FGs are, of course, excellent at this and do it as a habit anyway, but you should also expect it from your mate. Not calling when he will be late is a common failing among boyfriends – they couldn't find a phone, didn't think they'd be late, didn't know the time, whatever. You will have to sit them down if this behaviour is habitual and ask that your feelings be taken into consideration. This is not nagging but courtesy, and your partner needs to be made aware of the difference.

DID I SAY THAT?

Being part of a union requires flexibility. It's not possible for either member of a couple to go on behaving as they did in their single days. Prohibitions are necessary. These include sex outside the relationship, but they must also include some kinds of language. Consider the following to be off limits for reasons of etiquette as well as sanity:

1. 'Am I fat?' What can he say? He can't be truthful, and if he does confess that you've packed on a few since you met, will you ever be able to get it out of your head? It's hard enough to feel good about your body; don't ask other people to get involved with your self-image. If you want to be thinner, then do something about it. Better yet, accept your curviness – he probably does. If you can knock this phrase

out of your lexicon entirely, it's better. In any case, do not involve him in this issue, for both your sakes.

2. 'Do you love me?' If he loves you, he'll tell you. And that's what you want, right? To be told without asking. If you love him, tell him and see how he replies. You can only ask if it's been a while or if it's been bothering you to the point where you're considering a break-up over it.

3. 'Are you attracted to her?' Yes, he is. So what? Don't torture yourself or punish him for having natural, acceptable feelings for other women. If what you really want to say is 'It makes me uncomfortable when you leer at my friends', then say it.

4. 'How does this look on me?' Are you asking permission? Your wardrobe is your own business. Listening too much to a boyfriend's advice may lead you to overtly dowdy or sexy dressing.

ARGUMENTS

No couple, no matter how in love they are, agree on everything. How dreadfully dull it would be if that were true! While heated arguments are *de rigueur* for passionate screen couples, the Fabulous Girl, no matter her temperament, should learn to argue with civility. No raised voices, no throwing objects, no destroying your partner's stuff and no name-calling. And never, ever just ignore your mate because you are angry; giving him the silent treatment is childish, akin to that old playground whine, 'I'm not your friend any more'. Instead, wait until the object of your irritation is in the door and say a polite 'Hello, how was your day, we need to talk'. Chances are your partner will know that a discussion is in order too. Don't beat around the bush, this is frustrating for you both and will only raise temperatures. Just tell him the problem – 'I hate it when you answer your phone when we're out at a restaurant' (a very common fight) – and you can discuss it.

PUBLIC DISPLAYS OF AFFECTION

Affection should be location-appropriate. Dinner for two at a quiet spot? Go ahead and slip your foot out of your shoe and put it in his lap. Come back from the bathroom and place the tiny fistful of G-string in his pocket and quietly tell him about what's going to happen at home later on. But the well-mannered FG refrains from intense tongue-frolicking and body-stroking in a restaurant. Knowing you cannot behave this way only adds to the sexual tension that will explode later. On the bus or on the pavement, tone it down. If you're in a group or with a single friend be sensitive that your live sex show might not be appreciated.

PUBLIC DISPLAYS OF ANGER

We all know how uncomfortable it is to watch a couple grope and moan next to you on the tube while you sit alone reading *Emma*. The only thing more inappropriate than too much affection is too much aggression. Some couples clearly get off on getting carried away with arguments in public. Just like the amorous couple above, public fighters are really showing off the passion of their relationship. And of course, it's difficult not to pay attention to every barbed word being flung about by such scene makers.

If you are on the tube or in some other truly public place, there's little you can do. But if you're in a restaurant, you should feel free to do something about this intrusive behaviour. Ask the waiter to help you out or ask them to keep it down yourself. The couple will probably be embarrassed and hush up immediately. Or they will drag you into it or make you the new focus of their anger. Be the polite one and don't fall for it. Say your piece and get back to your table.

If you are the one finding an argument spinning out of control while you're standing in line at the cinema, put a stop to it. As soon as you realize you are raising your voices, make a plan. Either leave to continue the argument somewhere more private, or set a date to continue the fight later at home. You won't be satisfied with the outcome of the argument if you have to keep whispering and worrying about crying in public anyway.

Jealousy and the 'X' Factor

EXES ON THE STREET

If you and your man run into your ex on the street or at a party, you must promptly introduce the new guy to the old guy as if it were the pleasantest task in the world. Unless we are talking about a very recent break-up, you should also show some sign of affection to the new guy. Nothing overt – just holding his hand will do. And absolutely expect the same in return from him.

THE X

No matter how fabulous an FG is, and no matter how wonderful the relationship is, lurking in her mind is the knowledge that there once was a girl whom her boyfriend loved very much. This girl broke his heart. He almost married her. She's 'the one that got away'. She is not just any ex-girlfriend, she's *the* ex. And of course, the first time you meet her, you're having an FG day off, with the hair and wardrobe to prove it. But don't despair, be gracious. Ignore the fact that she ignores you but strokes your boyfriend's hair affectionately or keeps touching him during the conversation. Remember, he's going home with you. The only suitable form of revenge is to conveniently forget her name. Every time you see her, after she's prised her lips from your boyfriend's cheek, say confidently and with a bright smile: 'Hi, I don't think we've met?' This will drive her crazy and convey that she doesn't matter to you or to your boyfriend.

If, however, your beau is close friends with one or more of his exes, then you must learn to cope. Trust is vital. Your mate should make every effort to make the situation comfortable by inviting you along to dinners or movies with the ex-now-friend. During any moment of doubt, remind yourself that you are a Fabulous Girl and that any number of men would love to be with you, your current boyfriend included, so stop worrying. In fact, the less hassle you give Bingo when he's out for coffee with Fifi, the more you will be appreciated. If he makes every effort to keep you apart, then you may have reason to worry, if only because it illustrates his lack of manners – and an FG cannot live with that!

FRIENDLY FOES

It may happen that the ex-girlfriend is actually your close friend. The proper behaviour, of course, is that you discuss your attraction to her ex with her before you sleep with him, or at least before your first date. You are not asking permission per se, but you are extending her the courtesy of hearing it from you first. If it's comfortable for all involved, then there is little to worry about.

Your friend may initially feel awkward with your dating her former man – particularly if the break-up was her most recent. Give her time and space. Eventually she will move on in her life and then all of you can hang out. She may, however, not get over it, and how will that affect your relationship?

Even if you've tried to handle the situation with the utmost diplomacy, some people just don't like the idea of having their exes having relationships again. Or they don't want contact with anyone they're no longer involved with. Think carefully about what you might be giving up if this is the case. Thankfully, as people get older, they tend to be more reluctant to throw away friendships – even those that are complicated.

THE FABULOUS GIRL AS EX

An FG knows that she can be intimidating to her ex-boyfriend's new girl. Never expect that the new girlfriend will be an FG. She may be actually rude to you. The only civil thing to do is to ignore her rudeness and be gracious and friendly. When you are at a party with your ex, make sure you include the new girl in the conversation. Make eye contact with her and ask her about herself; don't just focus on your ex. If you are seeing someone new, now is a good time to mention it – it will allay the other girl's fears.

If, however, you are a broken-hearted FG, then gracious civility applies twofold. You want her to feel comfortable, and you also want him to think you're not still crying while clutching his picture to your chest at night. If you are still not over him, don't hover too long at his side or get drunk and try to be best friends with the new girl. Leave them alone. Avoid the dreaded drinking and dialling, and do not imagine them in bed together. If he really has a new girlfriend, it's time to burn the photo of you two at Christmas in Cornwall.

197

His Issues

Due to the FG's contagious passion for life, she will no doubt have a selection of admirers wherever she goes. This, coupled with her natural superiority at flirting, can send many a boyfriend into fits of jealousy. As any FG knows, a small amount of jealousy is very sexy. That slightly possessive hand around your waist after your boyfriend notices you hitting it off with new-man-in-town Vlad the actor is fun and will make him appreciate you and enhance that night's sex. However, there are signs that there is too much jealousy and that it may hinder the FG's ability to flourish:

1. He begins to criticize your wardrobe.
2. He begins to tell you what to wear.
3. He won't leave you alone to mingle at parties.
4. He asks you to account for every second you're apart.
5. He accuses you of being attracted to other men (which you probably are at this point).

This type of behaviour may mean that it's time to move on: no man is worth this stranglehold on your creative and personal expression.

Gift-Giving

Whatever kind of gift-giver he is while you're dating is exactly the kind of gift-giver he'll be as a mate. So don't fool yourself into believing that increased affection will parlay into better presents on holidays. And don't berate him for being lousy on birthdays if he always was. You must respond graciously to any gift, no matter what you think of the appropriateness of a blender for Christmas. No-one owes you a gift.

You can, however, analyse what gifts mean:

Clothing. Only confident men venture into the clothing

zone. If he wants to get you something, he'll probably call your best friend to go with him. If he does it alone, he deserves big time credit or boyfriend points, as he is risking a lot – not only because of the size issue, but taste as well.

Jewellery. Regardless of price, a gift of jewellery means he is very serious about you.

Gifts from his parents. This can be deceptive and does not indicate ardour on his part. His mother may just be dying for him to settle down, and by giving you a birthday present, she may try to draw you into the fold. You'll know this is particularly true if the gift is home-related or sexless, say, a chopping board or a flannel nightie.

Family and Friends

FAMILY VISITS

His family

A meeting-his-parents kind of event is where an FG shines. She can go to town with her best manners and charm, and everyone will, of course, love her. She can be comfortable in these situations, free from the suspicion of etiquette she may encounter at other events.

If he wants you to meet his family, then he's serious about you. Don't agree to meet them unless you are also serious. The older you become the more strict you need to be about this rule. You just don't need to do it unless there are going to be many more visits – family holidays, Sunday dinners.

No matter what the occasion is that brings you together, dress a little more conservatively than you normally would. It's not only a sign of respect to his family, but it will also put you at ease. Why put yourself through the stress of an afternoon spent wondering if your blouse is too transparent?

Shake hands. Be cheerful. Go with the flow of their household. If you're staying longer than a night or two, you must fit in with the schedule of the house you're staying in. Don't just offer to wash the dishes: do it. Help unload the groceries from the car. You don't want to add yourself to his family's lore: 'Remember the time that girl was here and didn't lift a finger?' Don't doubt it.

Your family

Meeting your family is a far tougher encounter. Make it short, and if you're worried, make a reservation at a restaurant rather than going to your childhood home. It can happen that merely being in the home of her youth can send even the calmest FG hurtling back into sullen adolescence.

Try not to sulk if your parents seem to like him more than they like you. Consider your beau as a kind of buffer between you and invasive questions into your personal life. Your mother's probably not going to press you about the prospect of grandchildren in front of the new guy, so enjoy this time for what it is.

Remember, you are responsible for your boyfriend's comfort. Don't allow your parents or anyone else in your family to quiz him or drag out the family Super-8 films of your school talent show.

If it does go badly, you need to evacuate immediately. Do not hesitate to book into a hotel if a family meltdown occurs while you're visiting. It's not fair to submit a new boyfriend (or an old one, for that matter) to family ugliness.

Don't hesitate to let your family know if their behaviour is inappropriate or making your guest feel uncomfortable. When families get together, they slip into very old and set patterns and may not realize that it's not everyone's idea of a good time to shout out abusive jokes or to rely heavily on sarcasm.

Family policies

Once in a relationship, you may want to decide as a couple what your family policy is going to be. If your mate spends every Sunday lunch with his Aunt Agatha, you are not obliged to come along. Once in a while, when your mate really needs your support during a gruesome family reunion, you should agree – if only to build up your own good-girlfriend points. But you don't have to behave as if the two of you are a single entity. Likewise, you should assume that visits with your family are something to be negotiated with your mate, not command performances. This may cause your family to wonder about your relationship. Secretly, though, your disbelieving relatives will envy you for not being caught up in the knee-jerk reactions to obligations that most people live with.

COUPLE FRIENDS

If you're lucky, your friends and his will get along with ease. In all likelihood, though, they will remain separate camps. (Which will become very clear if you break up). While you should be a good sport about going to his best friend's wedding, you don't have to learn to play golf and join him at the links with his old college pal every Saturday.

The compromise you must make is at dinner parties. Each half of a couple must be willing to entertain their mate's pals at DPs. At larger parties this is easy.

It will be obvious to your beau if you don't like his best friend, so you don't need to tell him. Graciously avoid time with his loser friends. And don't force him into a friendship with someone from your gang.

Living Together

MOVING IN

Forget about whether the toilet seat gets left up or down: the single most difficult issue facing a shacking-up FG is shared furniture. If you've lived alone or with flatmates for any amount of time before moving in with a boyfriend, then you have accumulated some stuff. And so has he. International-level diplomacy is necessary to navigate the coming together of his IKEA bookshelf with your grandmother's antique desk. A person's sense of identity is very much wrapped up in a sense of style, no matter how he might deny this. So be very gentle about commenting on his furniture.

You may truly loathe his things, but don't be too hasty with demands for a car boot sale to get rid of his collection of cartoon character beer steins. You may feel now that this relationship is the one. Odds are that this is in fact the relationship for right now. Do you want to be responsible for his having to start all over again furniture-wise when you break up in two years' time? It's rare for an FG to move in with a guy with stronger aesthetic opinions than her own, but it does happen. Don't give up your favourite chintz-covered armchair – and what it means to you – to fit into his über-modern sensibility. If one person dominates the making of aesthetic choices in the new digs, then it is not a truly shared home.

HOUSEWORK

You may be moving in with the most progressive man alive. In dinner party debates, he may consistently take a feminist position on all matters, but even when a so-sensitive-he-menstruates kind of guy moves in with a woman, ten points are immediately knocked from his IQ. Suddenly he will forget how to put away his own laundry even though you know he used to do this simple task all on his own. He will claim not to know such ephemera as which side of the plate the napkin goes on.

In the face of this sad reality, an FG must be very tough. Tensions and squabbles over household maintenance are the most tedious sort and must be nipped in the bud. Either sit down immediately and sort out a schedule and refuse to be moved from it, or feign ignorance of your own: 'Why, I don't know how we're going to have breakfast because someone put a centimetre of milk back in the fridge last night.'

In order to keep the relationship polite and civil, you may consider the following:

1. Have separate phone lines.

2. Divide housecleaning chores: be very specific!

3. Do the laundry together or be responsible only for your own.

4. Cook as many meals together as possible. This way no-one feels like a 'wife', plus it's very romantic.

5. Buy each other fresh flowers every week to brighten up your new place.

PETS

In succumbing to the urge to nest and 'settle down', many couples find that they are not complete unless they hear the patter of four paws. Whether it's a kitty or a puppy, a little ball of fur can lead to much strife if its presence is not truly a joint effort. FGs are animal lovers, and for some reason moving in with a boyfriend will make it seem that life is stable enough for a pet. So off the new couple goes to the dogs' home or pet shop and they romantically choose their new addition. However, it must be made clear that both of you want the animal. If as an FG you are determined to have that Great Dane puppy but your beau Bingo isn't keen, then he will take you at your word when you say, 'I will do all of the walking, playing, training and I will pay for all of the food, collars, leashes, vet expenses, etc.' Do not expect him to go for those 7 a.m. walks on Sunday mornings if he didn't say he would. If your pet choice was a joint venture, then both of you must take turns in all aspects of pet ownership: no squeamishness about picking up after your dog or cleaning the cat box.

You may carry on in this blissful manner for years, but if the break-up occurs, who gets the pet will be determined by:

1. who paid for the animal in the first place;
2. who takes the responsibility for pet care;
3. who really wants the animal;
4. who the animal prefers.

One of you must take on the charge as a single person – no dumping the poor thing back at the dogs' home. The height of ill manners is to abandon an innocent loved one!

If the cost of caring for your Great Dane now includes a dog walker or doggie daycare then your ex should help out. Yes, this is 'puppimony' or 'catimony', as the case may be, and it is gracious to offer and to accept. If you don't ever want to see your ex again, then one lump sum will suffice. Obviously very few exes are so forthcoming with financial aid, especially for pets. If he won't help, then move on and do it without him. Getting over the lout will be easy when you are confronted with such ungentlemanly behaviour.

KEEPING THE FABULOUS IN THE GIRL

One of the most difficult aspects of maintaining a healthy relationship is not losing yourself in it. When she falls in love, an FG may try too hard to love everything about her new man at the expense of her own individuality. She may, for example, eschew her friends and her art class for his mother and golf. An FG must make time for herself and her life. This means not being available to see him every time he calls. It means making dates with girlfriends and working on that short story collection that she's been scribbling out in her spare time. Not only will this keep the FG an FG, but it will enrich the relationship. He will appreciate her more not just because she isn't always at his beck and call, but because she still does all those fascinating things that attracted him to her in the first place. And if the romance sours, it is much easier to get her life back, since she never lost it to begin with.

MAKING PLANS

Always assume that your partner's time is as valuable as yours. When friends call to ask you over for dinner, ask him about his schedule before answering for both of you – even if you know he's not busy that night. Likewise, don't bring friends back to your place after the pub shuts without calling ahead to see if he's in the mood for a nightcap with the gang. It's also a bad idea to ask the friends who stopped by for a coffee if they'd like to stay for dinner before you've checked if your boyfriend had anything else in mind first. Obviously, you'd want to be treated with the same consideration.

GO YOUR OWN WAY

Although social pressure to marry and procreate when you are young has loosened considerably, there are still unspoken (and spoken) rules to which you may feel obliged to conform. And since the vast majority of people do conform to these rules it can be uncomfortable and lonely to be the weirdo who does not toe the line. Perhaps you and your boyfriend have a great live-in relationship but never intend to get married. Or you've always known that you don't want children. Or you sometimes take holidays with your best friend instead of your husband. These will probably seem like the most natural choices in the world to you, but these practices will, on some level, raise the eyebrows of those living a more conventional life. At times it may even seem to threaten them because they read your choices as a judgement on theirs. And perhaps there's some truth in that. Ultimately, though, the way you and your partner choose to organize your life is your business. Don't be bullied by the normal people.

THE COUPLE'S BALANCING ACT

Sharing your life with someone is a true art, and an FG is certainly a master. Never fall into the 'we' trap. You know who we mean – those couples who always preface everything with 'we', as in 'We always order the red' or 'We like the humidity'. Try to catch yourself and slip in a few I's along the way.

There are, of course, difficult choices that many couples face and that can tear them apart. Career is one. If both of you are driven, ambitious people, then this can be a tricky issue. Both of you will need to be supportive to each other at company functions such as the Christmas Party. But you can only reasonably expect your significant other to attend two such gatherings per year: they are a dreadful bore for anyone not associated with the company or industry. Of course if you are both in the same field, then it is up to the individual. When you are in attendance at your mate's event, he should not abandon you too long or too often, and he should willingly introduce you to all his colleagues. If the two of you have events on the same evening, don't pout – go alone. There should be little argument over whose function is more important; for example, between your book launch and his department's bowling night, there is no question.

As for extra-curricular activities such as sports or hobbies, we would all love it if our mates were as passionate about show jumping as we are. But although he may very well love horses, he might not want to come watch you ride every weekend or help you bath your horse. He may prefer to join his friend in a tennis match or to go scuba diving. If neither of you makes an effort to participate on some level in each other's hobbies, however, then it does not bode well for your relationship. If he doesn't like or respect how you choose to spend your leisure time, then that will eventually create a wide gulf of resentment. He will hassle you about all that time you spend at the stable, or you will grow to despise how he looks in a wetsuit. The polite mate will seek to learn about or appreciate what you see in what you do and be supportive.

All of these issues could also come under the general heading of time given to a relationship. If you live apart, then your expectations for day-to-day communications will vary according to your schedule. An FG may want to see her man once a week and on weekends, while he may want to see his FG every day. It is important to discuss what is comfortable for both; an FG requires balance and space to thrive.

If you live together, then it may be less of an issue, as you will see each other eventually anyway. However, do not become so complacent that you fail to tell your mate your plans. Include the significant other in your life, but also allow him the freedom to go out without you and try new things on his own.

Your boyfriend may get an amazing career opportunity that requires moving 3,000 miles away, thus forcing you to either break up or to quit your fab job and move. Much discussion will follow. If he is a gentleman, he will not assume that you can or would give it all up for him. He should give you options and time to think it through. Sacrifice is the true test of love. What are you willing to give up, and how much is he asking you to give up? If you can see moving to Glasgow as an adventure, then the sacrifice of your career is not too much to ask.

MONEY

Talk this over before you move in together. You can't assume you know how people feel about money and how it should be handled by romantic partners until you discuss it, so you may as well do it before the first bill arrives. There may be very little to talk about. You're each going to maintain your own bank accounts and split everything down the middle. But what if you've just had a windfall and the love of your life is still struggling at his entry-level position? Are you going to live in a cramped basement flat because you want to keep it even? Maybe. Or maybe you'll decide you're going to pay the rent and he can cover the council tax and water bills. Whatever, make sure you agree on something that you can live with now *and* later. Is it something that may leave you feeling bitter if things don't work out between you? Whichever side of a wealth imbalance you find yourself on, be sure that wealth does not equal control. The person who pays the greater share of the rent shouldn't become the boss. That's not sharing.

Breaking Up

Brevity above all. Know why you're leaving, and consider carefully what you can reasonably communicate to him about your choice to go. Remember, it is rude and mean to tell him he's a terrible lover or simple-minded; this type of detail will not make breaking up easier, can scar him and does no service to the FG.

If the relationship has been brief – six months or less – then the old standbys, 'I'm sorry, it's just not going to work out' and 'I guess I'm just not ready' are fine. Don't get drawn into a long conversation about it: do it and get out of there. And no matter how badly you feel about hurting him, don't try to go into pal mode overnight. It's confusing and unfair to the person who is getting dumped.

To make any break-up convincing, you need to keep your distance from the person you've dumped. If you're calling all the time or getting together for coffee, then you're still in some kind of relationship.

If the relationship has been longer – one year or more – you're going to have to get more specific about why you're leaving and you're probably going to need to have a couple of pre-break-up warning conversations. Let him know that you're frustrated by the number of arguments you've been having. This just makes the final break easier to explain. As in the under-six-months break-ups, you need to keep it as brief as you possibly can.

The most important but most difficult thing to say is that your feelings for this person have changed. It may feel nasty, but it's what he needs to know. He should harbour no illusions that if he just didn't own a motorbike or use the word 'pastiche' so often, the two of you would be happy for ever.

FACE TO FACE OR NOT

Not every break-up has to be done face to face. But if you are in a committed, exclusive relationship then in-person is the only acceptable method. If, however, you've been hanging out for a few weeks casually or haven't had sex, then a phone call to say that you've met someone else is fine.

The Fabulous Girl:

1. ends a long-term relationship in person;

2. refrains from speaking to the walking wounded for a minimum of two weeks;

3. doesn't suggest friendship unless she means it;

4. doesn't offer to introduce him to another woman to alleviate her guilt;

5. does not lay blame unnecessarily.

BEING DUMPED

It sucks. It always sucks. Even if you wanted out of the relationship yourself, it still sucks. It's worse, of course, if you are still in love with the person who is ending the relationship.

The worst – but completely understandable – impulse is to want an explanation for why you're being dumped. And, tragically, you need to hear it over and over and over to fully understand how this could happen. (In fact, many FGs can't get past the ego-assault of being dumped until they've had ex-sex. But more on that later.) Try as best as you can to resist conducting the Spanish Inquisition. Get as much information as you can at the moment: does he never want kids but knows of your desire for a family? Is he unwilling to make that essential move to Manchester with you? And think it over with your girlfriends later. If he's giving you concrete reasons like the ones above, consider yourself lucky. If he's not, then his heart has changed and you don't need to be reminded of it by asking him to reiterate his stance.

Never utter these phrases to your newly minted ex-boyfriend when you're being dumped:

1. Don't you love me any more?

2. Is there someone else?
3. What did I do?
4. Can't we try one more time?
5. I can change.

Some examples of I-don't-love-you-any-more-but-I-can't-bring-myself-to-say-it excuses he may use are:
1. We've grown apart.
2. I don't want to be in a relationship.
3. I need to focus on my career.

DRINKING AND DIALLING

It's best to avoid getting drunk at all in the first month after being dumped. You will, of course, be very much drawn to red wine in this period, but it's a very dangerous time to get even tipsy. The moment you feel that alcohol in your veins, you will begin to think that it is the perfect time to really get to the bottom of this whole break-up nonsense. You may even feel good about it, as in 'Hey, I'm having fun and feeling good – now would be the best possible time to call up my old pal the dumper and have a good old chat with him.' The next thing you know, you're bawling over the phone and asking him if you can come over to his place because you don't want to be alone tonight.

This attraction to the phone after a glass or two can continue well beyond your true feelings for the dumper, so be careful. There's just something about alcohol that releases every buried hurt.

If you've ever been on the receiving end of such a phone call, you know how terribly unattractive they are. And the last thing you want as the one who got dumped is to confirm for your dumper what a good decision he made.

Break-up return policy

The Fabulous Girl knows in her heart that she should return her ex's leather jacket after he dumped her. But it fits so well, and doesn't she deserve a token to remember him or a prize for her pain? Well actually, no, she doesn't. Once a relationship is over, it is time to split the goods, the numerous small items left at each other's homes during sleepovers: toothbrushes, pyjamas, bras, books, CDs, and all that. Wait a week for things to cool, then carefully pack up a cardboard box and set up a time to exchange goods. He should be equally forthcoming with your stuff.

Gifts given during a relationship should not be included in the box of your ex's belongings. Those gifts belong to the receiver, and tossing them in with the other stuff is only a silly attempt to hurt the other person and is generally done in haste. You may regret giving back that antique sapphire friendship ring. Likewise, neither of you can demand that gifts be returned (unless they are family heirlooms). If you really don't want something he gave you, then give it to charity or to a distant cousin where it won't be under your nose all the time.

Sex with your ex

If you have sex with your ex more than three times, you are back together. Doubt us? Go ahead, continue getting down with your ex and enjoy the 'What does this mean to you?' conversations that will promptly ensue. It is particularly bad form to have sex with the partner you left behind and think he or she will assume that it's only physical. If you're very lonely or merely amorous, try going solo. Remember, you asked to be single again.

Recuperative sex

As soon as you're able to get out of your misery outfit of tracksuit bottoms and his old rock T-shirt, you need to have sex with the nicest, best-looking man you can get your hands on. Casual sex with an attractive and sympathetic man will do wonders for your ego and remind you that there is life after what's-his-name. You can even let the lucky guy know what you're up to. There aren't many men who won't agree to be a party to your sexual healing. But don't spend the night talking about getting dumped; the idea here is to get your mind off it.

Ex-sex

It happens. You run into your most recent ex on your way home from a party when you're wearing a new dress and you've just had your hair cut. He can't help but notice what a fox you are while you're making polite small talk. You end up having a cocktail at a nearby bar, and damn if you don't keep bumping each other's knees and accidentally brushing hands. By last orders there's no doubt that you're not going home alone. And that's all fine, particularly if he broke up with you. It can be good for your ego to know that he still finds you attractive.

You shouldn't, for obvious reasons, have ex-sex too close to a break-up as it will definitely lead to all kinds of confusion.

And don't forget, you cannot have ex-sex more than three times in a year. If you do, at least one of you thinks you're getting back together.

Things were cooking along nicely until I noticed that Groovy seemed a bit depressed. He left after I did in the morning and came home early. In fact, he seemed to never leave the flat.

Then he announced one night, over a roast pork tenderloin, 'The film's been cancelled. For good.' He stared down into his plate. I placed my hand over his on the table. 'I'm so sorry, sweetheart. But what do you mean "for good"? I don't think you should give up on it.'

He looked up at me and said, 'I'm giving up on film altogether. I've had it with this life of waiting and being rejected. I need a big change.'

I nodded and tried to smile sympathetically. 'What kind of change?'

'I don't know yet. I need to take some time off to work out what I'm going to do next.'

I looked down at the stuffed pork on my plate and lost my appetite. 'So you'll have to live off savings for a while, that's not a biggie...' I tried to sound supportive.

He shook his head. 'There aren't any savings. All the cash flow I ever had has been lost on this project. You're going to have to carry things until I get on my feet again.' He seemed relieved to have shared his burden with me. Groovy stuffed his face. I suddenly wanted to tear the food away and put him on a diet.

But perhaps I was being insensitive. After all, we were committed to each other, and isn't part of a relationship the willingness to help out your partner? Wouldn't Groovy support me if I lost my job? I stared at him as he relished his free meal and I wondered: would he?

After three months, I realized that he wasn't all that anxious to get a job. He'd spend all day at Starbucks and read the paper or tour the local golf courses. All on my credit cards. He always remembered me, though. There would be a bouquet of flowers, a CD or a magazine. Of course they were all bought by me, but it's the thought that counts. Then the debt collectors started calling. They called on weekends, at night, at 7 a.m. Groovy would never take their calls. I became a spy, looking through his mail after he'd opened it. He was in debt. Major debt.

I thought I'd be smart-money girl and help him set up a budget. We sat down and I told him my plan. He was furious. 'You have no right telling me how to manage money. I'm a grown-up. I'll get out of debt my own way.'

'How?' I asked. 'Do you expect me to pay them?'

He stood up and paced. 'Don't be so insensitive. I thought we had a commitment. If you don't want to stand by me, then maybe that's it.' He stormed off.

I had to think about this. What had become of my fabulous life? It finally came to my conscious mind that I had been miserable for the past two months because of him. He had taken over my flat and my money. Enough was enough.

'I think you should move out.'

Somehow a month later it hadn't worked out that way. There we were, Missy, Eleanor and I, packing boxes into a van and moving me into Missy's place. Kitty meowed in protest at being in a cage on my lap on the drive over. I began to bawl. 'Men are bastards,' was the wisdom of the moment.

What had happened? Simple: as soon as I told Groovy to vacate, he became unbearable. He wasn't going anywhere; if I wanted the relationship to end, I'd have to leave. He was committed to 'us', and that meant staying and seeing it through. He somehow managed to get a job working on Bingo's teen TV show. But his very presence became intolerable. I looked at him naked in bed and wanted to puke. The very thought of him touching me aroused only dread. Still he didn't leave. Bit by bit, day by day, he and his faux relationship zest drove me out. I couldn't take it.

Missy offered her second bedroom to me and I jumped at it – cowardly, yes, but a battle over a rented flat just seemed undignified and I desperately wanted to be single and fabulous again. While we were unpacking, Missy got a mysterious phone call. She was all coquettish and even blushed when Eleanor and I quizzed her after she hung up. 'Just this guy I met.'

'At the restaurant?' I pressed.

'He was a customer. Yep,' was all Missy would admit to.

'Maybe all men don't suck?' prodded Eleanor. Missy shrugged and heaved another box up the stairs.

Weddings and Divorce

Suddenly Missy was the coolest girl in the universe. Our best friend had, in six months, gone from Jill Job waitress to fiancée of the most handsome, nice and stable guy ever. His name was Joe. He had taken one look at Missy and her little apron and fallen in love. He came to have lunch or dinner at her restaurant five days a week. Of course Missy had to finally ask him out, but from then on he took courtship to new heights.

So there we were, Eleanor and I, decked out in bottle-green sateen bridesmaid gowns complete with spaghetti straps and frou-frou crinolines. It was Missy's wedding day. So we had to be ugly.

'I thought Missy was our best friend,' I said as I tried to crush the tank-size crinoline down in front of the church mirror.

'Not after this. Really, is this the mark of a friend?' Eleanor asked as she lowered the matching pillbox hat onto her head. 'I look like a leprechaun in drag,' she sighed.

Hideous dresses aside, Eleanor had other reasons for sulking. Bingo and she had split for the last, and we all hoped final, time. I knew she wanted to be happy for Missy, but poor El was miserable.

Missy blew into the church looking ravishing in a white, Jean Harlowesque gown. 'You both look so glamorous,' she hissed. Our sweet Missy had become the devil bride. She had done nothing for the past four months but obsess over every detail of her confection of a wedding, describing the difficulties of planning an event as if she were the first woman ever to put on such an extravaganza. Eleanor and I had secretly considered standing up during the ceremony to announce that the wedding couldn't take place due to Missy's having an incurable STD. In fact, during that crucial moment, I had to clutch Eleanor's hand hard to ensure her silence.

Outside, the pictures were being taken and we, of course, had to pose for our share of them. 'Doesn't she realize that wedding pictures will last for ever?' I asked Eleanor, planting my hat further down on my head.

'No matter what you do, you can still see it's you,' hissed Eleanor, through gritted teeth.

Missy ran up to us beaming. 'Well?'

'It was magical,' scoffed Eleanor and trounced off.

'What's wrong with her?' Missy asked.

'I think her hat's too tight,' I offered. But the truth was that while Missy was the devil bride, Eleanor was winning awards as the bride's bad best friend. She had helped me throw the engagement party, which, proudly, we did in true grown-up party fashion. We opted for Manhattans at the Orbit Room, a groovy, cavernous jazz club, for the three of us and fifty of the bride and groom's closest friends. But Eleanor couldn't be counted on to be a gracious co-hostess that evening because she and Bingo were in the midst of their break-up and breakdown. Luckily the jazz quintet was loud and brash enough that the guests were spared the yelling and tears. Honestly, almost no-one noticed. Except, of course, Missy. 'What does she think she's doing?' she demanded.

'I think they're breaking up. Again.' I, too, was un-sympathetic. After all, how useful was a co-hostess in tears?

Missy said, 'This is my night. Dammit! I'm going to say something.'

Before I could stop her, Missy had stomped over to the raging couple. From where I stood, it was like watching a silent movie – accompanied by a raucous jazz band, mind you. All I could do was to try to decipher the angry faces and flailing limbs.

Missy pulled Bingo and Eleanor apart and seemed to be lecturing them as if they were bad children. Bingo tossed down his glass, its smashing sound smothered by a trumpet solo. He stormed out. Eleanor screamed at Missy, but the beaming bride-to-be gave as good as she got. Eleanor then stormed out, leaving me to pay for the broken glass and soothe Missy.

Of course they made up the following day, everyone agreeing that pre-wedding and post-break-up nerves were to blame for the fight. But now I was stuck balancing elation for Missy's happiness-ever-after and compassion and outrage at Eleanor's state of disunion. And that left me alone to defend Missy's choice of china against Joe's preference, help convince Missy's folks that the wedding wasn't too expensive and defend Eleanor's bad behaviour. It also left me unable to fend for myself in the case of the ugly dress.

At the reception I had the honour of toasting the groom. I was so nervous about speaking in front of 200 people that I was nearly sick.

'I wasn't happy about Missy getting married,' I began. Missy started to frown, so I knew I had to hurry up and get to the point. 'I wasn't happy because I knew when Missy announced her engagement that things would never be the same between us again. She's been one of the most important people in my life in the past ten years and I can't imagine ever having a better, more loyal friend. So, you see, that's a hard thing to share with anyone – other than our other best friend, Eleanor, that is. But when we met Joe and saw how he loved our Missy, we had to give in. If anyone is allowed to usurp our position in Missy's life, then I couldn't be happier that it's Joe. In the time that we've known Joe, Eleanor and I have decided that he's up to our standards and, most importantly, appreciates what a beautiful, loyal, funny, smart and fabulous woman he's marrying. And so, while we realize that Missy's dad has already walked her down the aisle and officially given her up, Eleanor and I want you to know, Joe, that we too give you our whole-hearted blessing. Here's to Joe.'

Of course Missy cried and that's the main thing.

Here is where life got weird. For the second dance I was paired with the best man, Mr Nice Guy – tall, handsome and polite. He asked me about myself. He'd read some of my pieces and was impressed. His excellent manners made me swoon. For the first time in my life, I was not repelled by a nice guy. He didn't seem wimpy to me; he seemed attractive. This fact alone worried me, but I kept dancing. When the song was over, he graciously said 'Thank you', walked me back to my seat and left me standing there with my heart racing.

Missy appeared out of nowhere and squeaked in my ear, 'I need you and Eleanor in the garden for more pictures'. I knew what that meant: I would get to stand close to Mr Nice Guy. Somehow my enthusiasm for the wedding accelerated and I almost raced Missy to the garden. Eleanor, however, was nowhere to be found. Missy and I searched and were horrified to find her snogging a teenage cousin of Missy's in the bushes.

'Eleanor!' shouted Missy. Eleanor let go her grip on the boy and looked at us, none too ashamed, and then simply wiped her hand across her lipstick-smeared mouth. She was very drunk. 'The photographer is waiting,' Missy stammered.

'Can't you see I've met someone special?' Eleanor defended herself. Missy's under-age cousin shifted nervously, trying to wipe away the leaves that were sticking to his suit.

'It's my day, not yours!' Missy's face was purple with rage.

While my two best friends fought agonizingly over whose selfishness should rule the day, I couldn't help but think that both of them were being ungracious, and I wanted to put a stop to it, if for no other reason than to join Nice in the garden. 'Both of you shut up!' I shouted. Me, who never raised her voice. I noticed how effective it could be. Both women were silenced. 'Missy, it is *your day* officially, but that doesn't mean you can order us around like servants. For the past four months, you have been a self-absorbed brat and demanded our undivided attention without any thought about us.'

Eleanor looked triumphant. 'And *you*, Eleanor – I know you're upset about Bingo, but really, now is not the time and certainly not with someone who isn't even old enough to drink. Though he's probably drunk from your breath. Behave yourselves. Badly done, Missy. Badly done, Eleanor. Now let's go find the photographer and get shot.' I stood my ground while the girls filed past sulking.

Weddings

Despite all logical arguments to the contrary, some FGs decide that they have found their one true love and decide to make a splashy, lifetime commitment to them in public. Perhaps she had a lot to drink just before he asked her. In any case, she's said yes, told her best friends and her mother and now the wheels are in motion.

ENGAGEMENT ETIQUETTE

More often than not, the man will select the engagement ring he likes and thinks his future bride will like. If he is smart, he will have solicited opinions from his girlfriend to aid in his choice or have sought the company of her best friends during the buying. If, however, the ring is not to your liking, then it is wise to tell him. You may not, however, ask him to exchange the ring just because you want a bigger or showier stone. Engagement rings are meant to be tokens of love, not, as some greedy guts believe, a financial measure of your worth to him. Wait a couple of weeks to see if the ring grows on you and then be gentle but honest. Be careful how you phrase it, though, as this is surefire argument material.

If you call off an engagement, you should return the ring. This is particularly true if the ring was his great-grandmother's or the like. If, however, he is the one who turns tail and runs, then you are not obligated to return the ring. To keep it can feel yucky and simply be an unpleasant reminder of your break-up, however, so it is wise to sell it. To make a truly grand statement, donate the proceeds to charity.

WEDDING PLANS

There is no other event in an FG's life that arrives with quite so much historical baggage. Even the most cynical woman has grown up in a culture in which getting married is seen as one of the single most important finishing lines to cross. It takes some very level-headed thinking to remind yourself that a marriage is a beginning, not an end in itself.

Well, you did it. You've said yes and now you must handle the whole thing with as much grace as you possibly can. This will not be easy. Everyone and their dog will be getting in your face between now and your nuptials: your mother, his mother, your great-aunt Beatrice, his cousins from Prague who can't possibly be asked to stay at a hotel and more.

Make a decision with your mate (remember him? Yes, we know, you'd already forgotten about him) in the very beginning: are you going to do this your way, despite the pressures of your families? Or are you going to go with the flow and give everyone else the wedding they've always wanted?

Either decision is perfectly fine – just be sure to make a decision. Nothing is more tedious than a bride who halfway through her wedding preparation hell starts complaining, 'I didn't know everyone would get so crazy'. This is completely unacceptable, and the people around you may have to slap you. Weddings are emotionally, culturally and financially loaded events in which everyone close to them goes crazy, every time.

Even if you and your mate do decide to run the show yourselves, you can still involve your families. Ask your mother to oversee the sending out of invitations and to monitor the RSVPs. Ask his parents if they would mind researching reasonably priced hotels in your area where out-of-town guests might stay. Ask your maid of honour to keep track of who gave what gifts. Delegating in this manner does not mean that you are giving up control.

Above all, though, remind yourself in the middle of the pre-wedding chaos that everyone in the world is not as engaged in this event as you and your family are. The wedding may become the very centre of your world for the next few months, but all the people around you will carry on with their lives.

MONEY

Weddings cost a lot of money. Stylish weddings can cost a fortune. How many weddings have you been to where you can tell that they spent tens of thousands and it still looked like a meringue exploded? Even small affairs cost a lot more than a comparable event that isn't bridal in nature. Flowers cost more, dresses cost more, photographers cost more. It's not fair, but it's true. You and your mate need to sit down and talk about what you're willing to spend and what you are willing to let other people spend on you.

Accepting large sums of money from your parents or his can mean giving up control, because when people pay for things, they start to take ownership of them. It's natural. This will come up first when you are designing a guest list. You may have it in your mind that you'd like a very small wedding, just family and your closest friends. If your dad is footing the bill, though, he's going to be thinking about how Fred from the office invited him and you mum when their daughter got married. For most of the world, a wedding joins a couple to God, to their families and to their community. They therefore feel that members of all those groups should be in attendance at your wedding. Be prepared to be really tough if you do not feel the same way about it.

In many families, money is difficult to discuss. These are things that must be decided, however, before the money is actually spent.

RESPONSIBILITY

You may be marrying the most progressive man alive, but he will not want to talk about china patterns and he will not put as much work into your wedding as you will. Think about this carefully.

You should have a very frank conversation with your mate about how much time he is willing to put into your wedding. He may tell you he is willing to spend three hours a week on wedding-related chores. You can then decide if you, too, will spend only three hours per week and thus determine how complicated an event it will be. In the end, you may decide that you really want the whole big deal and that you are willing to pick up the slack yourself or delegate it. No-one else in your life will be expecting him to lift a finger over the wedding. Not your parents. Definitely not his parents. Nobody. This is entirely unfair, but true. It's far better to figure this out in advance rather than halfway through all the work when you start to resent the hell out of your mate for not equally pulling his weight.

WEDDING LISTS

Registering a wedding list is a very common practice. The argument for it is that it saves people worry over what it is you need. For very young couples it's a useful way of acquiring the basics they don't have: plates, bedlinen, towels, a toaster.

However, there is something crass about telling people exactly what gift it is you want. What it says is that you want to ensure that you're going to like the gifts you receive – that in fact, you want to pick them yourself. You will come under pressure to provide a list, though, as it does make life easier, particularly for people who don't know you well or who don't see you very often.

If you are over thirty, registering for gifts seems even more greedy than it already is. You probably have, between the two of you, all you need, so you're trading up. Some couples ask that gifts be made in the form of donations to favourite charities.

Think carefully about the cost of things on your list. Yes, you want to create a list of items you actually want and need, but do also consider that your guests may be on different budgets. Are there things on your list that your cousin the medical student can pick up for you? Don't make every element on your list an item that you couldn't afford on your own.

YOUR DRESS AND THEIR DRESSES

You've been thinking about it for a long time, this dress. If at all possible, don't buy your dress at a typical bridal boutique. Faced with the racks of bright white meringues, it will be difficult for you to remain objective. Suddenly the least frothy number you try on seems like a winner when really it's only a tiny bit less egregious than the others.

Know any designers? Having a dress made is not necessarily any more expensive than buying one. The cost of wedding dresses can run very much higher than comparable non-bridal evening gowns.

Consider a suit. Consider a colour. Consider that you'll have those pictures for ever.

When it comes to the bridesmaids' or maid of honour's dresses, be as generous as you possibly can. Everyone is well aware of the history of bad seafoam satin off-the-shoulder numbers that have been inflicted on perfectly nice women. Some unkind, if honest, brides will admit that they just don't want anyone stealing their thunder on the big day. This is both selfish and silly. Everyone is looking at the bride no matter what anyone else in the room is doing. So why not allow your friends to look as good as possible? Remember that they will appear in your photographs too. The worst example we know of this nasty need to be the ultimate princess involved navy blue palazzo pants made of layers and layers of pleated chiffon. This is a true story. Really, is this the act of a friend?

Good taste is particularly important if you are asking your girls to pay for their own dresses. Try as best as you can to pick something they can wear again. And don't just say it, really do it. Shift dresses suit many figures and can always be worn again. If you don't think your bridesmaids are going to remember how you treated them in this regard, think again.

LOCATIONS

You may have always dreamed of getting married in your childhood town in the country, and your family may be delighted by your choice. If you've been living in London, though, think about the expense that your choice will mean to your current group of friends. Perhaps they are all wealthy and would love nothing better than a weekend away. But for many it will either be impossible or mean that your wedding is their only trip away for the year. If your friends do not feel that they can afford to make such a trip, you must not hold it against them. Let them know you'd be thrilled to have them there but that you also realize you are asking a lot.

If friends and family are coming a great distance to be with you on your big day, then you must take responsibility for them. Research hotels (of differing costs) or establish which families might accommodate guests. Make up a fact sheet about your wedding location that includes the addresses of good restaurants, shopping, sights and entertainment. If you give people more reason than just your wedding to come a long way, they will travel the distance more happily. You aren't responsible for being with them during their stay, but you are responsible for offering them suggestions about how to spend their time.

INVITATIONS

Wedding invitations should be sent out further in advance than other invitations. Give people at least six weeks' notice. If you are asking them to travel, make it eight weeks. And definitely give them an RSVP date so that you're not panicking about the caterer the week before your wedding. If you do not receive replies by the date specified on your invitation, it's fine to follow up with phone calls (or ask a good friend to do it for you).

Don't take it personally if invitees are late in replying. People get a great deal of mail, and of course, you are not the centre of their universe. You do need to know how many people to expect, however, so go ahead and harass them a little.

Your invitation should be clear about what you are inviting people for. Your wedding, of course, but are they also invited to the reception after? Only the reception? Will there be dinner? The food part is particularly important, since people want to know if they should show up hungry or fed. And if you can't afford to provide an open bar, definitely let them know. Also give some kind of indication of the level of formality you are expecting.

So:

Miss Fabulous Girl
and
Lucky Guy
request the pleasure of your company at
9.30 a.m., 29 June 2000,
for their country wedding at the cutest
little church in Cute Town.

A champagne breakfast will be served
at the Charming Country Inn at 10.30 a.m.

Please, no gifts.

An invitation like this lets people know when, where and what is going on and gives them an idea of what they should wear. Of course, close family and friends will probably ignore the gift part, but you will gain points for having included it.

Under no circumstances may you invite people to your wedding by e-mail. Even if crayons and cardboard are your only means of paper invitation within your budget, they must be sent by mail. E-mail may be used to gently remind people that they haven't sent back their RSVP.

You do not have to invite everyone you work with to your wedding. Send invitations only to those you really want there. You do not need to explain to others why they have been excluded, and it is poor form for them to ask or harass you for an explanation. If you are compelled to alleviate any ill feelings, simply tell the person that you have only limited space.

THE RECEPTION

You are obliged at your wedding reception to make an effort to chat with as many people as possible. If you had some fantasy of this being a party where you and your new husband could dance the night away looking into each other's eyes, forget it. While you are not necessarily the hostess of this event, you do have to try and spread yourself around. (Sort hostessing out in advance: is it you hostessing? Your parents? His?) First, there is often the receiving line where you, your new husband and your families stand in police-line-up formation to shake the hands of everyone you've invited. You must also stop by each table, if you have this kind of set-up, and have a brief chat. This is particularly important to do with your new family. In many cases, this will be the first time that you're meeting Lucky Guy's Uncle Ron, so go over and say hello and thank him for joining you on your big day.

Going away

You may be having so much fun that you want to stay until the end of the party. You are not obliged to. It's perfectly acceptable to leave long before the rest of the party breaks up. You can change into a going-away outfit – many newly-weds leave the wedding directly for their honeymoon – but you can also make an exit in your gown.

Make your getaway a quick one. Just be sure to thank all the parents and the members of your bridal party before you zip off.

Thank you

You must send your thank-you notes as soon as you're able to. Thank-yous are a task a couple should share. Remember to thank people both for their generosity and for sharing the day with you.

Post-wedding

No matter how careful you have been about these things, your friends and family are going to be sick of you for the next couple of months. So if your birthday or your husband's birthday falls six weeks after the wedding – or just before – forget about asking people to show up somewhere with gifts and cheer. Keep a low profile for a year.

One bad friend

At nearly every wedding a bride will have her sisters, her sister-in-law-to-be or her best girlfriends with her as her bridesmaids and maid of honour. And one of them will let her down. Ask anyone who has been married: there's always one girlfriend – and you can't always guess which one it's going to be – who screws up. She's late or just doesn't show up for the rehearsal. She doesn't want to stay at the same hotel as everyone else. She doesn't want to help you out of your veil because it would tear her away from the guy she has just met. She ends up dirty dancing with someone else's fiancé. These are all real-life examples of bad bridesmaid behaviour. Maybe she's jealous. Maybe she just can't see how stressed out you are by the prospect of a party this size with everyone looking at you. And since you are at a party where you are the centre of attention, you just have to let it go. You can't get into a confrontation, so don't let it bother you. Go and dance with your husband instead. Remember him?

Calling off the wedding

Second thoughts? Carrying another man's child? There is nothing to be ashamed of in calling off a wedding if you know it's a mistake. Not enough women have the strength to quit while the wedding engine roars at full throttle. Forget about the money, the gifts and the disappointment of friends and family. This is your life.

Tell your parents and be firm. Then it is their duty to make a simple announcement by telephone – or in person if you're at the church already – and cancel the arrangements. And yes, the wedding gifts do have to be returned, with brief thank-you notes.

ELOPING

Remember, there's nothing more chic than running away and coming back married. It may annoy people in the short term, but they'll get over it, and you can always throw a party later.

YOUR FRIEND IS NOW A W-I-F-E

If you are the unmarried FG, you must realize that there will be a period of adjustment for your newly crowned wife friend. She may be in the honeymoon phase for the entire first year of her marriage. She will have less time to see you than before. And because she is married, she may be less inclined to see you without her husband.

The issue of changing her name may have come up before the nuptials. Whether or not you agree, you must respect her decision. Unless you are close friends, never ask a woman why she took her husband's name, and do not scoff or sneer when she announces that she has. It may take you a while to call her Mrs, but if that's what she wants, it is disrespectful not to. Likewise, do not harass a woman who intends to keep her own surname. And don't worry, her future children will be just fine no matter what their last names turn out to be.

CROSS-CULTURAL WEDDINGS

Multiculturalism has been spoon fed to us from an early age. How these theories work in reality becomes apparent when Ms Mohammed marries Mr Yang. What's a girl to do? The time and place to decide whether two individuals of differing cultural and religious beliefs can make a perfect union is during courtship. Once engaged, one of you needs to give a little, and often it is the person with the least strict beliefs. The question of religious conversions needs to be answered before nuptials.

As a guest attending a wedding not of your own culture, you must respect the differences. The bride and groom should consider a typed list of what can be expected as an explanation to guests not familiar with their customs. This is helpful, not insulting, because many people won't know how to correctly hold their hands during Muslim prayer or how much money to place in the collection box at an Italian wedding.

Divorces

The Fabulous Girl may not find married life suitable for her independent spirit. If stifled and smothered by an uncompromising husband, she may bolt for freedom. Divorce is a rite of passage for many people, whether the Moral Majority like to admit it or not. A significant number of marriages end before death. Many, in fact, feel like mortality itself. Nonetheless, as countless FGs will have to navigate the inner turmoils of guilt, failure and loneliness that characterize separation and divorce, they should do it with proper decorum.

ASKING POLITELY

If the FG has firmly established that she cannot carry on in her marriage, then this needs to be stated. Unlike common-law relationships, when despite their legal obligations most couples can split up without going to court or hiring lawyers, a divorce is serious business. An FG needs to ask for a divorce, not demand it (unless the husband has been having affairs or is in any way abusive). If the reason is the very common 'growing apart' or the ever-popular 'irreconcilable differences', then asking is polite.

It is very likely that both of you are unhappy. Never assume that the misery is one-sided. After exhausting the marriage counsellor, a trial separation is a natural next step and helps both of you to gauge how you are on your own again.

There is no easy way to explain to a spouse that you want to leave them. Expect to feel terrible. Even if you want a divorce, suggesting separation first allows the spouse to feel some hope. This may seem unfair, but it's kinder and in fact allows some breathing room in case during separation you change your mind and realize that you want to continue in the marriage.

EXPLAINING

Of course your spouse will require an explanation. Again, do it calmly, this will give the appearance that your decision has been well thought out and is not a desperate attempt to cause pain during a heated argument. The FG does not pick fights to end a marriage, but she may cite constant sources of disagreement in order to back up her decision. It is then polite to leave the other person alone for a short period. Go for a walk, or better, go for a drink with your best friend. You cannot be a comfort to your spouse at the same time that you are the source of the pain. Let him grieve in private.

MOVING ON

Flaunting a new lover in front of your ex or soon-to-be-ex is impolite. Chances are that one of you is still smarting from the divorce. Propriety calls for discreet encounters. We're not implying secret rendezvous, but rather not inviting the cute boy from the car wash to a mutual friend's cocktail party when you know your former husband will be there. The well-mannered estranged couple does not discuss new relationships unless there is something to be told. If one of you falls in love, then by all means your ex should hear it from you first, but if it's casual dating, then 'Oh I had the date from hell on Tuesday' is the last thing he or she will want to listen to. After all, you may have been friends during the marriage, but breaking up requires distance and neither of you should be privy to the other's re-emergence on the single scene.

LEGALITIES

If you decide to move ahead with divorce proceedings, a lawyer will be necessary in most cases. It is considered very badly done indeed for one of you to engage a lawyer without prior notification of your intent to do so. This is akin to a declaration of war, and once this gauntlet has been thrown, the chances of an amicable divorce are greatly reduced. Instead, the polite to-be-divorced FG informs her husband that she will be seeking legal consultation and may suggest he do the same.

ANSWERING TO A HIGHER AUTHORITY

This means your mother. It matters little if an FG comes from a broken home or from the Waltons – a divorce may prove your mother right: that he was bad news or that you are incapable of commitment. Such rants are difficult to avoid. Mothers-in-law may also feel compelled to call with their tuppence worth or to tell off an FG for hurting little Timmy. Ignore them all. Do not engage with the mothers unless they can be reasonable and agree to listen to your side. Quite frankly, it is none of their business. Some families, for religious or other moral reasons, cannot accept divorce: 'There's never been a divorce in our family. Can't you forgive him for sleeping with your sister?' If they continue to hound you, then make quick goodbyes and hang up the phone or leave the house. There is something to be said for the British stiff upper lip. Save your grief and tears and ranting for a select few, not just anyone with an ear.

OTHER PEOPLE'S DIVORCES

Due to the supportive nature of the Fabulous Girl, she will no doubt be one of the first people a friend will call to announce that her marriage is over. It is perfectly acceptable to be and act shocked – but only so far. If it truly is a surprise, then say so, but then listen, do not ask. Above all offer your company in person, right away. She or he may need a person to confess all to. Offer to tell other mutual friends the news; the estranged person may not feel up to hearing what everyone has to say. Which leads to the next thing: reactions are vital here. Never say, 'I knew he was no good' or 'I could see that coming' or 'To be honest, I'm not surprised', even if all of that is true. If that is your opinion, wait for your friend to ask for it; don't offer such criticism unless solicited.

PARENTAL SPLITS

A Fabulous Girl may have two parents who are still married when she enters adulthood. However, they may have been waiting for you to land that partnership before breaking the news to you: Mum and Dad despise each other. You of course will be devastated, and all those images of fake holiday kinship will explode before your eyes. But deep down you knew they weren't happy.

You have to be supportive, but it is tricky. Suddenly you will be thrust into the parental role with your parents as the children, needing your unconditional love and support. Of course being children, they may not play fair; they may call each other names and not want to play in the same sandpit or share their favourite toy: you. This is unacceptable. If parents behave badly, be firm. Remember all those times you were relegated to your room? Tell them that they can tell you their side, but that you are going to be on good terms with both of them. You may well need to encourage your parents to look for support elsewhere. Let them know that while you want to be helpful, there are other people in their lives who can give them more than you can. Be honest with yourself about how much mum-bashing you can take from your dad (or dad-bashing from your mum). Let them know you expect both of them to be able to be in the same room at future events, such as your wedding. Unless someone was abused, there is never any reason that two adults can't be in the same room at a social event.

The next stage of their life will also involve a switching of roles. Once they get back on their feet, they may no longer need their Fabulous Girl daughter to be a parent, but they will want her as new best friend. Yes, this may mean that your mother or father will want dating advice – including, of course, condom choice and romantic weekend breaks.

Depending on your relationship with each of them, this will either be distasteful or a hoot. If it's uncomfortable for you, then tell your mother or father that you cannot be that kind of friend for them. If it's fun, then indulge them and give them the same tools you had when you started out.

A couple of weeks after the wedding I started dating Mr Nice Guy. He was so, well, nice. No temper tantrums, no whining, no moodiness. He called when he said he would. He didn't get anxious if we spent several days in a row together. I'd never realized how easy a grown-up relationship could be.

But a major test was about to begin. Could he cope with me under stress? We were snuggled up on the sofa watching *Pride and Prejudice* when my phone rang. It was my father: 'Your mother and I are getting divorced.'

I was stunned. I hadn't spent that much time with them lately, but I'd never suspected anything was wrong. He assured me he was fine. I insisted he put my mother on the line. 'I'm fine, dear,' she said. 'It's very amicable.'

Amicable? Both of them agreed that splitting up in your fifties was a good thing? They may have been fine, but I wasn't. I spiralled into depression, wondering how I could have caused this, thinking back to how little time I spent with them. Maybe it was my fault for being inattentive; they felt they had no purpose in being together.

Then Mr Nice Guy sat me down and told me what to do. 'Have dinner with your parents – separately. Hear them out about what happened before you reach any conclusions. I was only fifteen when my parents split up and wasn't able to work out for years that it wasn't my fault. I wished we'd just had honest conversations about it.'

I took Nice's advice, and what emerged was that both of my parents were ready to move on and find new partners for the rest of their lives. They'd been unhappy for many years and had finally decided to act on their feelings. I tried to elicit innuendo or intrigue or betrayal from either of them, but it really did seem that they had their heads on straight and that I was the bitter one. After each dinner, I slumped on my sofa and waited for Mr Nice Guy to comfort me. He did. Having gone through the same thing himself, he knew that in the end parents were just two people with needs like ours. But he also didn't fault me for being upset by the whole upheaval. Well played, Mr Nice, I thought to myself.

Of course, Missy's marriage had also meant yet another move for me. My next place was in a converted loft building. Not one of those pretend lofts that are really studios. This had actually been a place where an artist had lived and that some kindly developer had renovated and made more profitable. And Kitty and I were settling in nicely, thank you very much.

The furniture situation wasn't perfect (the furniture G.G. and I had bought together seemed to have been left with him in my haste to get out of our relationship), but I had all the basics covered: futon (but no frame yet), Eleanor's great-aunt's bridge table for the kitchen (and four, count 'em, four, matching chairs), a love seat that I covered in a purple and gold sari, two IKEA bookshelves, a really crappy stereo and a black and white TV. Oh, and Kitty had her own chair. You were welcome to sit in it if she wasn't there, but only her small weight didn't make the seat nearly crash to the floor – so really it was all hers.

It was probably in reaction to her own divorce that my mother felt the need to give me Granny's china. When I will ever be in need of a full set of twelve of everything I can only guess. When we talked on the phone, it was like she imagined another life that I might be leading, one in which I had exactly three magazines fanned out on the coffee table, guest soap sitting unused by the bathroom sink and potpourri lying desiccated in bowls throughout the flat. Then she came over and looked around, disappointed. The day she delivered the china was like that.

'What you need really is a hutch or something to display it in,' she said as she looked around, frowning. I was feeling a little annoyed by it all. I mean, I'd already taken *The Joy of Sex, Fantasex*, and my illustrated copy of *The Kama Sutra* off my shelves so as not to disturb her vision of me entirely.

'A what?'

'A hutch. It's a cabinet for displaying things in the dining room.'

'Well, I don't have a dining room either, so...I think I'll just leave these in the boxes until I work out what to do with them. I do really love it, though. Thanks for bringing it over.'

Then she started picking at my collar. 'Don't you have an iron? We'd better go out and get you an iron.'

The phone rang. Rhonda said, 'Hey! It's me, and you'll never guess where I am!'

'Hey, you're in Paris, right? Or did you get transferred to Rome?'

My mother was taking the opportunity to sneak into my room. Which was fine, since I'd actually made my bed and put away any egregious little accessories.

'I'm in Paris. At the airport. I'll be there in three hours!'

'You're coming home? That's so great. Are you staying with your mum?' My own had been in my room for far too long.

'No, she's too out of the way. You don't mind if I crash with you, do you? I hear from Missy that you've got your own pad now. It'll be such fun.'

'Wow,' I said. 'Well, it's quite a small place really. And it's sort of all one room because it was a studio before.'

'Oh! They're calling my flight, I'd better run. See you

soon! Do you think you could meet me at the airport?'

'My car is at the garage. Can't you take a cab?'

'Yeah, I suppose. Doesn't that friend of yours, Eleanor, drive?'

'Yeees, but I don't know if I can really ask her to drive out there, Rhonda.'

'I guess I could take the bus. I'm a little low on cash, you know?'

'Well, I guess I could ask Eleanor...But how will you know if we're going to be...'

'I'll call you back in ten minutes so you can call your friend and ask.'

'I thought your flight was being called.'

'Oh, they'll wait. Bye, sweetie, you're the best.'

And that's how Rhonda came to stay for a month. It wasn't so bad, really. I just decided that I still had a flatmate and that my independent life would really start when she finally got on a plane back to Paris. Although she didn't exactly pitch in for groceries or do much in the way of cleaning, she did end up spending most nights at her ex-boyfriend's place. Usually I would advise a girlfriend not to indulge in ex-sex for an extended period that way, but I admit in this case to selfish motives. Rhonda kicks in her sleep and I was happy to have the futon to myself on the nights she was having self-destructive sex.

I didn't really notice how much time Nice Guy was spending at my loft until well after Rhonda left. If you'd asked me, I would have said he only stayed over twice a week, but honestly, it was probably most nights. After the disaster with G.G., I just couldn't face the thought of cohabitation. Even with someone as perfect as N.G. I finally twigged to how much a part of the place he'd become when one Sunday afternoon Kitty climbed into N.G.'s lap for her post-lunch nap. She writhed around there for a bit while he petted and scratched her and complimented her on her beauty, and then she fell deeply, contentedly asleep. Well, who wouldn't?

I'll admit that my first reaction was panic. What's next? Kids? Too much too fast. Just like G.G. But you have to trust your pets. If Kitty was OK with it, why shouldn't I be? That's why I offered him a drawer that day. And I felt really quite grown-up about it – not quite ready to shack up again, but quite grown-up.

Home

Regardless of her income bracket, every FG's pad should be a palace. Maintaining an attractive and comfortable home is essential in the life of a Fabulous Girl. Definitely not a mark of conservatism, her well-kept home is instead a reflection of her fabulous nature.

You can't always control your environment during the work-day, but your home is where you are in control, even if you're not rich. So as much as you're able to, take advantage of it. Take the time to paint your walls a pleasing colour. Spend what you can on furniture. Buy yourself fresh flowers. Keep your home clean and tidy. Think about cleaning and decorating your place the way you do about exercising or eating well: it's about looking after yourself.

Flatmates

There's a period in every FG's life – as long as ten years in some cases – during which flatmates will be a fact of life. Flatmates are great: shared housing makes urban living possible and oftentimes fun. They're also a nightmare: you never get any privacy, and you have to tolerate their terrible furniture. Even if she is your closest friend, and especially if she's your best friend, you must establish ground rules.

Three key areas can become contentious: boyfriends, food and clothes – not necessarily in that order. Decide on a policy.

If your boyfriend is spending three nights or more per week at your place, then he is also living with you. And that's one more body using the hot water, eating the cornflakes and going through toilet paper than you and your flatmate had planned on. They may resent Bingo being there around the clock. Ask her how she feels, or get Bingo to buy food or con-tribute in some other way. If all this seems unreasonable, then perhaps you should think about living with Bingo.

Decide how you feel about shared groceries. Are you going to the market together every week and splitting it all evenly, or are you the label-on-your-jar-of-strawberry-jam type? Either way, decide and act on it. If you are cooking dinner and your flatmate comes home, it is polite to offer her food. If she takes it, then she must return the favour and cook for you some night. This can be an unspoken law of the land, but it should be followed. After all, what's the point of having a flatmate if you eat all your meals in your room?

And then there's clothes...Even if she says her wardrobe is your wardrobe, ask every time you want to borrow some-thing. And return it, washed, immediately. She won't care until she finds her third-date dress in a heap on your bed-room floor just when she needs it. If either you or your flatmate is not of the sharing persuasion, those limits must be respected.

PRIVACY

Living in a shared house can mean a lack of privacy. You never know when you're going to have the living room all to yourself or when the bathroom will be free for an hour-long soak. You'll also find it difficult to organize a romantic evening for you and your lover. When you are in the living-with-flatmates phase of your life, your lovers are likely to be in the same situation. Most of the meals you and your sweet-heart will share will also be shared with the other people in your life.

There are few times when it's appropriate to tell your flat-mates to clear out, but the need for a rare romantic evening is one of them. You must give everyone lots of notice and ask them if they're willing to clear out on Friday the 12th so you can make a special dinner for your boyfriend's birthday or your anniversary. You may make this request only rarely. If you want to be alone for every meal, you must go to your room or get your own place. If you do make this kind of request, you must also be willing to give your flatmates the same kind of space in return.

HOSTING WITH OR WITHOUT FLATMATES

If you wish to host a dinner party that does not involve your flatmates' friends, then you must invite your flatmate as a guest and cover all the expenses and labour for the dinner yourself. If you do involve your flatmates in the planning and expense of the dinner, then they must be allowed to make half the invitations. You may not ever have a dinner party (except for the above-described romantic dinner for two) that excludes your flatmates.

What the Fabulous Girl Needs

THE MOST IMPORTANT SPACE IN AN FG'S HOME: THE WARDROBE

If you can, purchase a few good pieces every year, but there are certain items an FG cannot live without in her wardrobe:

The little black dress (always buy a new one every year). You may try to convince yourself to add more colour to your wardrobe, but nine times out of ten, this is what you'll feel like wearing.

A great pair of black trousers, with a straight leg and flat front, that falls below the ankle bone (when you have the money, extend this collection to include boot-cut, capris, etc.). When buying any style of trouser, your priority should be finding well-fitting trousers. Trousers can, like no other garment, cause distress and disappointment. A perfectly good day can be ruined at its onset by the pulling on of a pair of ill-fitting trousers that make you feel fat. Why do it? Never buy trousers when you're in a hurry or having a thin day. It doesn't pay. Get to know which styles – back pockets, hipsters – suit you and stick to them. Do not be moved by saleswomen who say, 'But you have a great shape. Emphasize it!' Yeah, right. That pair will end up never worn, in the back of your wardrobe. When you do come across trousers that give you a good feeling about your body, buy two pairs if you can. Again, nothing makes your day like trousers that flatter you.

A white, tapered-waist cotton shirt à la Audrey Hepburn.

A skirt suit. This should be a suit that reminds you of what a smart girl you are. Spend as much as you reasonably can. Take your time choosing it, and err on the side of conservatism if you can only afford one suit. As you can afford to, add to your serious wardrobe by investing in trouser suits also.

A dress you can meet his parents in (or for some other similarly uncharted territory). It may seem like an un-fun way to spend money, but you'll be glad you did. The problem is that as an FG, most of your clothes are stylish and current. When you are suddenly thrown into a more conservative milieu, it's possible to feel uncomfortable in your regular clothes. This is the rare time when an FG does not wish to attract attention. For these occasions, you'll be glad for your old faithful. Navy is better than black. To the knee. No cleavage.

Sweaters. Start out with classic shapes such as crewnecks and turtlenecks. You need a couple of good black sweaters before you need colour. Cotton sweaters can be the most comfortable but will not last as long as wool. Add cashmere and mohair to your sweater wardrobe for texture when you can afford it.

A good winter coat. Don't fool yourself about how you look in the winter: this garment is what you're in most of the time. It's hard enough to feel attractive when dressing for snow and slush; make it easier on yourself and put as much money as you can into your winter coat.

Shoes. When you're starting out, you'll need one pair each of flats, heels and boots that can be polished up to a decent shine. Add to this Kitten heels for trousers and skirts, ankle- and knee-high boots with a heel, mules, slingbacks and sandals. You need at least two pairs of shoes that don't hurt your feet, including one pair of heels that don't hurt. Of course you have lots of shoes that hurt your feet. Wear them to cocktail parties – or better, dinner parties. Let anyone you're going out with know that you won't be doing any walking. Jump from cab to door. But for long days or nights when walking can't be avoided, you need a few pairs of sensible shoes or very expensive heels. Unfortunately, with shoes, it's true that the more you pay, the better the fit and balance.

An assortment of bags: tote for work, beaded for evening. Bags can be very expensive, and you may not be able to afford a good one for several years into your adult life. A smart, good-quality leather bag gives a woman polish like nothing else (well, shoes are kind of the same that way, actually) and is well worth the money once you have it.

A collection of colourful scarves to prop up your basics.

At least three sets of matching bras and knickers. These must have some kind of decorative lace or embroidery. Of course FGs have countless practical/period underwear and bras for most days, but this does not diminish the necessity of grown-up lingerie. Every year you must build on your lingerie wardrobe.

It's also a good idea to have a few sex outfits. These can vary in style and detail and they needn't be expensive. A cheap, silky nightie that barely covers your bum is perfect. It only has to be worn briefly – the time it takes to light some candles in your bedroom and lie back is about it.

A good dressing gown. Something you can feel attractive in when you get up to pee in the night.

With these staples in her wardrobe, the FG can then go for fun and trends whenever she feels so inclined.

Bedside table

Condoms, obviously.

Nail file. The quietness of the period before sleep is somehow always the moment when you realize that your ragged index nail has been driving you bonkers all day.

Lip balm. There's nothing more irritating than being forced out of bed by dry lips.

The book you are reading. Usually a novel. Don't stop reading books – non-fiction is fine, but fiction is even better – or you'll become a terrible bore.

Alarm clock.

Vibrator. What did women used to say at those Seventies consciousness-raising sessions? 'I am responsible for my own orgasm'.

Lamp. No trips in the dark getting from the switch by the door to your bed.

A candle and some matches. Yes, everyone does look better by candlelight.

MEDICINE CABINET

Tampons/pads
Aspirin
Plasters
Cotton buds
Toothpaste and dental floss
Cotton balls
Antihistamines
(can also double as sleeping pills if you're
having trouble getting to sleep)
Rennies or Settlers
Antiseptic

FRIDGE

Milk
Dijon mustard
Butter
Juice
Vegetables
Fruit
Olives
Capers
Tonic water
White wine

FREEZER

Ice cream
Ice cubes

BAR

Whisky
Red vermouth
White vermouth
Vodka
Gin
Angostura Bitters
Brandy
Red wine

In your first apartment, you may only be able to afford a bottle of wine when you're expecting guests. As you get older and your bank account grows (we hope), wine should be the first alcoholic drink you keep regularly; most people drink it, and it can be consumed at most hours of the day. Once you're able to keep a fuller bar, move next to whisky. Brandy is useful in many cocktails and in cooking, so you may want to keep a smallish bottle at hand. If you want to be able to make mixed drinks, keep gin, vodka, red and white vermouth and – critically – Angostura Bitters (you can't make a real Manhattan without it). If you have a particular taste for liqueurs and bitters, go ahead, but a bar is certainly complete without them.

HANDBAG

Purse
Mints, not gum
Your cards
A pen
A small notebook
Lipstick
Lip balm

Your mobile
Sunglasses
Chequebook

CD RACK

A boxed set of jazz standards
At least one classical composer of your choice
(Mozart is always a good place to start, but try to
move on as soon as possible)
The rest is according to taste

BOOKSHELF

- *Oxford Concise Dictionary.*
- *Fowler's Modern English Usage* or other grammar text.
- Atlas.
- Art history.
- A history book that moves chronologically through time is useful.
- Novels should comprise the bulk of your bookshelf. Reading novels will make you a better, happier person. Reading will also give you confidence in the world of sensitive and educated people – the world in which FGs live.
- Complete works of Shakespeare.
- King James Bible. This version of the Bible is the one most often referred to in English literature.

Housework

It often takes an FG a few years to get into a housework routine – not because she's lazy or slovenly, but because she may feel resistant to such a retro role for herself as that of homemaker. FGs do well to get over this hang-up as they mature. While it's true that keeping a maniacally clean home is not as important as the other projects in your life, it is important to your well-being and worth doing well. You simply get more pleasure out of living in a cared-for house or flat.

If you share your living space, then figure out what the group standard is and have everyone agree on how the house will be maintained. This doesn't have to mean a silly chart tacked to the fridge, just some consensus as a group about exactly what level of tidiness is acceptable to all. If you are an obsessive cleaner but live with three more casual pals, you cannot very well insist that everyone adjust to your standard. Likewise, one slob cannot rule the lives of a group of neat freaks. You can always move.

It can be helpful to occasionally try to look at your place as if through the eyes of guests. It's very easy to stop seeing the stack of old newspapers piled up by the back door if they've been there for the last six months.

Most smallish homes can be kept tolerably hygienic with daily tidying and weekly cleaning. At a minimum, keep your kitchen and bathroom clean and every other room tidy. Your goal is not perfection but comfort. The tidier and more pleasant your home is, the more welcoming it will be at the end of your long day.

You may at some point in your life be able to hire someone else to clean your home, but until then, try to see housework as quiet, meditative work rather than as a chore you will grow to resent.

Decorating

If cleaning maintains your pad, decorating really makes it your own. Whether or not you've got lots to spend, you can give your place personality.

In your first couple of flats you will have to rely on posters to decorate the walls. Try covering shabby furniture with great sari fabric or something equally bright and beautiful. The cheapest thing of all can make the biggest difference: candles in quantity give a room an atmosphere that its contents don't necessarily generate.

Once you're well out of your college years, posters must either be framed or moved into a study – at your advanced age they're no longer living-room worthy.

Start thinking about what kind of aesthetic you want to develop in your home. You may feel that picking and choosing is out of your reach when you're still at the stage of accepting hand-me-downs, but it's never too early to start thinking about it. If you know how you feel about kilims versus Persian rugs, you'll know what to do when you spot a great deal at a flea market. Figuring out your own taste will stop you from making expensive mistakes with the little money you have.

Flea markets and antique stores offer lots of fab finds. Whether your taste runs to mahogany and other rich woods or to Sixties kitsch, you may be surprised at the amount of inexpensive furniture that can be found without too much effort. Decorating magazines should be studied in the same manner that you use *Vogue* for fashion. The more you know, the better and happier you'll be with your choices. An FG cannot go wrong with an eclectic mix of furnishings.

As for art, try to avoid buying original pieces simply because they match the sofa. Instead join the local art gallery or spend time touring smaller galleries to familiarize yourself with the works available and their artists. Art is meant to provoke thought and emotion, not to coordinate with IKEA.

House Guests

The home of the Fabulous Girl is indeed her palace: she is the Empress of her surroundings. Her art work, her books, her photographs all indicate her good taste. Then Mum and Dad visit. This alone can send her into a frenzy of good housekeeping prior to their arrival. But an FG must also decide how much of the real her she wants to reveal to her doting parents. It is wise on certain occasions to edit one's home in order to prevent strife. While this may seem old-fashioned, remember that the goal of the FG is gracious manners and elegant living. It may also save her from an unpleasant evening spent knowing her family (or whoever) is looking at the offending object in disgust. If you absolutely know Mum won't understand the painting of the masturbating priest, then hide it. Likewise, that artful nude self-portrait, sex toy or erotic poetry collection may be better off in a trunk by the bed while dinner is going on. While we expect friends and colleagues to respect our taste, somehow parents can make us doubtful, so editing is the best policy unless you can handle and accept their remarks, or unless your folks are civilized enough not to comment.

For a new lover, it is wise to remove photos of ex-boyfriends, no matter how cute they are and no matter that they will surely make the new man recognize what a catch he has.

How to be a hassle-free guest

Most people assume that others welcome visits by their loved ones. This is a delusion – a warm-hearted delusion – but a delusion nonetheless. The truth is that humans are creatures of habit. And very little throws off the comfortable habits of a human more than the arrival, and the setting up of camp, of others in their habitat.

When relying on the kindness of friends and family, whether you are couch-surfing in a pal's one-bedroom or inhabiting the empty wing of your aunt's summer home, the role of guest comes with a set of duties. Although several helpful rules are listed following, the key to being a desirable guest is persuasion. Let your actions and demeanour be a form of persuasion so that your host finds your stay a pleasant diversion rather than the imposition it likely is.

We cannot recommend strongly enough that you not make surprise visits. Although the well-mannered friend will no doubt put on an act of being tickled by your phone call from the airport ('You're at the airport! Of course you can stay with me as long as you want'), an act it most certainly is. Not only are you disrupting your friend, but you're also offending her by implying that she has no life to disrupt. This is a very bad idea.

For the welcome, anticipated guest, a balance must be struck between a delight in the company of her hosts and an independent, adventurous interest in the local sights. A visit that is weighted too heavily on either side is doomed to stress both the guest and the host.

Remember that while you are on holiday, your hostess is, in almost every case, not. Not only will this affect her availability for outings and late nights, it will mean that her state of mind is completely different from yours. She's slightly distracted by this morning's conversation with her agent. She's got to pick up her dry-cleaning, make a doctor's appointment and drop off some receipts at her accountant's. These vexations are magnified tenfold if your hostess is a freelancer of any sort.

A great guest arrives with a gift. Bring a bottle of Lagavulin single malt or the latest Will Self novel (or better yet, *Mrs Dalloway* by Virginia Woolf, a must-read for every hostess).

Immediately put your bags away, and for the rest of your visit, keep your belongings out of the way.

After the initial greetings and visiting, get the information you need to so you can get yourself out of the way. Get a local transport timetable. Pick up the paper to check gallery listings. Most important of all, though, is to understand and respect your hostess's schedule. When does she have to leave for work in the morning? Does she have any plans that necessarily exclude you? Find out how much time she can spare for skiving off with you. Likewise, don't hesitate to let your hostess know what you are particularly keen on doing – 'I really want to check out the Damian Hirst show' – while you're in her town.

If you pal seems irritable or in need of some privacy, turn in early one night and read in your room or go out to a movie on your own. If she and her boyfriend are having a row, make yourself scarce. And do your best to be deaf and dumb until she asks you for your advice.

On your way back from the gallery, stop in at the supermarket and pick up something great: a couple of steaks, a barbecued duck, a bag of perfectly ripe peaches. Such offerings make a contribution to the household you are staying in without slighting your hostess's ability to care for you. Don't, for instance, bring home milk and eggs unless you are planning to whip up a batch of French toast the next morning. If your visit is to last more than three or four days, it is appropriate to make a more basic contribution to the larder.

Make dinner for your hostess at least once. Wash the dishes on the nights you aren't making dinner. Take her out for dinner on your last night.

Send a thank-you note.

If these considerations seem too much to ask of you while you are on holiday, remember that you could always be free of them by paying for a hotel.

VISITORS

Aside from overnight house guests, an FG will receive company into her home frequently and will visit her own friends too. There are a few details of which all should be aware. Never answer someone else's telephone unless you are expressly asked to. Don't open the fridge or help yourself to food and coffee unless invited to.

Cooking

Although living in a city provides you with many opportunities to avoid cooking, an FG still knows her way around a kitchen. As with housework and hostessing, cooking may seem like an old-fashioned pursuit. And on one level, of course, it is.

But learning to cook and to enjoy it is also liberating. It's far less expensive than eating out. You control what you're eating when you prepare your own food. And although you aren't always cooking food for others, cooking for yourself and/or your flatmates builds your self-confidence for the times when you are cooking to impress. But most of all, learning to cook is one more way that an FG makes her world a more pleasant place.

Great pots and pans and other kitchen utensils are impossibly expensive for most people when starting out. Buy a cheap set to make do, then gradually, for birthdays and Christmas, ask family members (mothers in particular will understand) to buy the specific kind you covet. Good knives are the thing that will change your cooking experience the most, so start here, learning how to keep them sharp with a knife steel or stone. Collect these and other high-quality kitchen gear as you grow older. There is no hurry, and the good stuff lasts a lifetime. Besides, adding to your collection will be a nice treat to yourself when you have extra cash. Once again, do research to determine your preference for aluminium, cast iron or copper pots. Many cities have restaurant supply stores where you can get heavy-duty gear at a better price.

What you really need:

- A couple of small, sharp paring knives. These are perfect for peeling fruit and vegetables.
- A butcher's knife with a solid handle (if you eat meat).
- A stone or a steel to keep the butcher's knife sharp (see above).
- A serrated bread knife.
- Two or three mixing bowls; metal are easier to keep clean than plastic, but ceramic are the prettiest.
- A small Teflon frying pan, of a size you can comfortably fry two eggs in.
- A larger Teflon frying pan.
- A small saucepan for boiling eggs or heating milk.
- A medium saucepan for heating pasta sauce or making smallish quantities of soup.
- A large pot for boiling pasta water in.
- At least two cutting boards.
- Tongs for moving meat or fish around a pan or a grill without piercing it.
- A spatula.

Once you've got these basics covered, you may want to start building up the things you need to bake: cake tins, biscuit sheets, and so on.

Slowly build up a small library of cookbooks and work your way through them. Every kitchen needs *The Joy of Cooking* or some similar basic tome. It's not fancy, but it contains lots of technical information and basic recipes that are a good way to start. Depending on how interested in cooking your parents were, it's also a nice idea to get them to give you your family's recipes. Spend a Sunday writing down your mum's best curry recipe or your dad's excellent recipe for cabbage rolls.

After you've got a handle on the basics and on the family comfort foods that everyone needs to know, branch out. Follow your interests. The *Larousse* is an excellent source if you like French food. Marcella Hazan is considered to be one of the best writers on Italian cooking. Madhur Jaffrey's Indian cookbooks are authentic and easy to follow.

Don't psych yourself out. Try making a recipe two or three times before deciding if you want to add it to your dinner-party repertoire. Cooking is, in some ways, like learning a new language: it can take time to master the subtler points. After a while you'll start to notice that *tarte tatin* is harder to pull off on a humid day. And that egg whites just don't want to stiffen in a less-then-immaculately clean bowl. And some things like to be fried in a Teflon pan rather than in cast iron.

When disaster does strike (steaks that are uniformly grey instead of pink in the middle with perfect searing marks), who cares? It's one meal and there are many more to make.

Music

Listening to music is a pleasure on its own and also makes work pass more easily. When living in the city, music must be played with concern for those living nearby. Although an FG's taste is always excellent, she must admit that it might not be that of her neighbours. Always consider the sound-conducting qualities of your walls and what is passing through them. This is particularly true in the evenings when people are most likely to be at home. Of course many people now work from home, and so the volume of your music should not be high even during a weekday.

If someone complains about the volume, you must turn it down even if you think the complaint is unreasonable.

You must never, ever play music outside. Not in the city when you are washing your car. Not at the cottage when you are assembling your new barbecue. Never. The outdoors are necessarily shared spaces and since there is no way of assessing agreement on music (other than at, say, an outdoor concert where everyone has actually agreed on the music they want to listen to), it must not be played.

Buying Your First Home

There will, we hope, come a point in the FG's life when home ownership is more than a possibility: it's a reality. After years of renting and sharing life with hundreds of others in blocks of flats, the thought of your own home is sublime.

Shop around for estate agents before deciding who to sign up with. But trust us: you'll need one. A great one will save you time and money, respect which areas you'd live in and what your price range is and then show you only what you want. Some agents are notoriously pushy. Don't be intimidated. And by all means bring a third party along with you. A friend is good for aesthetic advice, but a parent or older relation may be better for assessing value.

Try to get a pre-approved mortgage so that there is no heartbreak when you've found the home of your dreams only to be rejected by The Bank. Make sure you have a down payment that is yours; do not borrow your down payment from a credit card. If you must borrow, ask parents or some other family member first. This will ensure that you have more capital and less debt to stress over.

When you own a home, you are responsible for everything, so remember your staff of people. Those handymen and plumbers will be the keys to your sanity in emergencies.

Budgeting

The Fabulous Girl may not always be fabulous with money; like a majority of women, she may have a terrifying love-hate relationship with economics. She needs to overcome her fear of money and her secret fear of growing old as a bag lady. Some women are so fearful of their lack of financial acumen that they avoid looking at bank machine receipts or opening their bills altogether. Learn to look money in the eye. Even if it's a struggle, make up a budget. Keep all your receipts for everything, even milk from the corner store, and tally them after each month. Do this for three or four months and you may see a pattern forming. Assess what was essential and what was frivolous. An FG needs frivolity to be happy, so don't punish yourself by deciding not to go out with friends for a whole month. But you may cut costs by trimming your magazine budget for instance. Buy the essentials, but remember that you can always lounge at the local Borders and read the ones you don't absolutely need. Try to set a certain amount aside each month and stick to it. Open a savings account and place this extra money into it. It is wise to set a 'buffer zone', for example, £1,000. If your savings account is £1,000 or less, then you have no money. Anything above it is free and clear. If you ever lose your job or need repairs to your home or car, you have rent and such taken care of. Make an appointment with a financial adviser at your bank, even though you think you don't have enough to bother with. If you've got a bank account, then those annoying service charges you've been paying entitle you to as much time and advice as your wealthy neighbour. Don't be afraid to ask for simple explanations of financial jargon. It may seem like a pointless endeavour to invest your lowly £25 a month. It isn't. It's an important habit to get into and it's also vital to feel in control of your financial future.

'*I just hate it when I have to wait around here*
while some workman is doing stuff in my place.'

'Why? Do you think they're leering or something?'

N.G. and I (and Kitty, of course) were doing my
favourite Sunday thing of reading the paper and eating
breakfast in bed. And I get first choice of the sections
because N.G. is so gallant. He also has very warm feet and
doesn't mind when I rub my freezing toes up against his
toasty ones.

'It's not that they're inherently lecherous. It's more that
they treat me like a student or something.'

'Why don't you mention your husband?'

'And who would that be? I've not met this husband of
mine.'

'It's this thing my friend Lucy does.'

'Lucy. Lesbian Lucy?'

'Yes. When she has to have something done to her house,
she mentions her husband while she's on the phone making
arrangements,' said N.G., putting down the Arts section.
'She says that she notices a difference in the way she's
treated when she creates this husband – who's never there,
obviously – and it makes her seem more, I don't know,
more respectable in their eyes.'

'That's so sad that she has to do that.'

'Yeah, but she doesn't mind. She'd rather do that than

have the electrician trying to work out what the deal is.'

'Hmmm.'

'And when we move in together – not now, I know – then I can call the plumber. Like a husband.'

Kitty forced her entire head into the milk jug, trying to vacuum out the bottom. N.G. pulled it off her face saying, 'Bad Kitty, you'll get stuck in there.' And then he patted my knee through the duvet. 'Don't freak out, now – it's just talk.'

I snuggled down into the covers, slipped my hands under his T-shirt and felt his nice, warm skin. 'I'm not freaking out. I'd be proud to have you as my pretend husband.'

Entertaining

After so much fun living like a grown-up, I decided it was time to brave that much feared social rite of passage: the dinner party. It was after N.G. and I had attended half a dozen of his and my friends' soirées that I first thought about it. And then one day after stubbing my toe on the box of china my mother had given me, I knew what had to be done.

Carefully I selected a menu of crab cakes, lobster bisque, scallops sauteed in shallots and white wine with grilled asparagus and roasted red pepper aïoli. The fact that I had never made any of these dishes before didn't faze me.

The day of the party arrived. I had invited seven people over so there would be eight in total: Missy and Joe, Eleanor, a couple who worked at the magazine and one of N.G.'s friends, a man I didn't know very well who came for the free food and the chance to meet Eleanor. N.G. offered repeatedly to co-host, but I turned him down. I wanted this to be my evening, my proof of being an adult living alone fabulously, and besides, I didn't want that nagging cohabitation feeling again.

Dinner was at 8 p.m. My guests arrived promptly and I began to mix drinks.

'Who wants a martini and who wants a Manhattan?'

'Oh honey, don't do both, just make us all the same,' offered Eleanor.

'Of course I can make both, *Eleanor*. Or anything.'

'Can I help in the kitchen?' Missy asked. Did no-one think I could handle things?

N.G. arrived and began to mix a few drinks himself. By that time I was thankful because the couple I knew from work had brought their two-year-old daughter Daisy with them. I was horrified. I hadn't expressly asked them not to bring Daisy, but honestly, who would bring a child to an adult party without asking in advance?

'I've got the drinks covered, why don't you begin dinner?' N.G. suggested.

'I can't now. I have to spend time with my guests!' I snarled back.

The CD had ended, but I couldn't care less because I had to spend too much time running after Daisy, who kept trying to grab little things off the shelves.

'You really need to childproof your place. She gets into everything,' laughed her mother.

'She's a holy terror,' giggled her dad as he crossed his legs and sipped his drink. They had decided that my dinner party was their holiday from parenthood.

'Now, Daisy, you shouldn't grab a wine glass. It doesn't belong to you.' I gritted my teeth.

'I'll watch her,' N.G. said.

Missy followed me into my open-concept kitchen and whispered, 'Is there anything to eat?'

'Of course. I just have to make it, that's all.'

'No snacks?'

'Could you go and find some music...'

Just then I heard the most awful howl and I dashed into the living room to see poor Kitty's tail, bent and twisted in the grip of Devil Daisy.

'Let go of her!' I ran over, but luckily Eleanor had untangled Kitty's fur from the brat's hand and Kitty had skittered under the bed.

'She's fearless of animals,' Daisy's mother stated proudly.

It only got worse. I hadn't even chopped garlic or shallots before the guests had arrived, and soon I had a room full of drunks and no dinner. As I stood there frantically chopping and sautéeing, I could hear N.G. trying to be funny and entertaining. But I could also hear a sarcastic battle going on between Eleanor and the eligible bachelor.

'I'm telling you, I always know when a woman is attracted to me. And I can tell that you are.'

'I hate to burst your bubble, but you're wrong this time.'

'You're playing hard to get, but don't worry. I like being hard too, you know what I mean?'

'You are a disgusting arsehole, do you know what I mean?'

This last sentence of Eleanor's was heightened by the abrupt ending of the Moby CD at the hands of sticky-fingered Daisy.

'OK, who wants crab cakes?' I spluttered. It was now 10.30 p.m.

People sat down to eat. Silently. I couldn't even look at N.G. We ate our meal without a word between any of us. I picked at my food, no longer hungry; the cocktails had killed my appetite.

I was very thankful when after my soggy scallops and runny aïoli people started leaving almost immediately. It was midnight. I wouldn't let N.G. stay over. I needed to be alone to contemplate my future as a hostess.

The Zen of Hostessing

The term 'hostess' may strike you as too retro for our modern FG, but nothing could be more hip now than taking on this age-old role and making it cook. The key to hostessing is frame of mind. Forget the image of you greeting your guests in a ruffly apron. Instead think of yourself as the very place where people come together. Of course you also have to look after people too – get them drinks, make your place comfortable and stylish, play the right music and so on. But above all, be happy about your task. People love to be looked after, but only by someone who wants to do it. There's bad karma in grudge entertaining (only having people over when you owe them for three dinners).

THE WORK OF HOSTESSING

Having parties, big or small, is work. As the hostess you must expect that you won't have as much fun as your guests. It's your job to make sure everyone's got a drink, to pass around food (and keep it going as the night proceeds), to listen for when the CD stops and most important, to get people talking. You must introduce people to each other and if they need it, get them started in conversation.

Avoid introductions by career, especially if people are from very different economic brackets.

A party is not the time to have a long, serious conversation with an old friend. Nor may you be out of conversation because you're in a corner with your new flame.

The Guest List

Whether you're having people over for cocktails, dinner or a bash, take the time to consider your guest list rather than just inviting the same list of pals you call on every time. The best hostesses develop a reputation for creating events that put new people together.

Mix up people from different fields; make sure to invite a balance of men and women (unless there's a specific reason not to); ask old friends and new. Don't be afraid to invite people you've just met or know only a little. In fact, this is often the key to a successful party.

Consider who are the debaters and who are simply decorative and diverting; put them side by side.

You should, at least loosely, keep track of to whom you owe invitations. You cannot expect to be invited if you are not reciprocating invitations. This shouldn't become a duty, but keep in mind that if you want to be a part of a social world, you must contribute to it as well as enjoy it.

You also needn't entertain in the same manner that you were entertained. If you want to 'pay back' Miss Super-Rich for the elaborately catered dinner she invited you to, it's perfectly gracious to ask her over for chilli and midweek football. Remember, it's the gesture that matters, not the cost of it.

Invitations

It is quite common and acceptable in our current cultural climate to invite people to a dinner party by telephone. However, the proper method is by written invitation. This formal approach is a rarity indeed in our hyper-paced time, but it can add an air of elegance and anticipation that guests will appreciate. It is not acceptable to e-mail invitations to a formal dinner party. E-mail invitations belong solely to casual get-togethers. They're fine for when you're meeting the girls for after-work drinks or a movie, but a dinner or cocktail party requires something more stylish.

The Dinner Party

For many, the dinner party represents the Rubicon of entertaining. It is essential to get over these feelings of inadequacy and do your part. If you expect to be invited to dinner parties, you must throw them yourself. It's all part of the social web.

AMBIENCE

Lighting and music go a long way to creating an inviting atmosphere in which guests can converse and relax. Candlelight works the best and should be your first choice. Groupings of pillar candles of various heights, widths and textures are ideal when set about the rooms like small still lifes. Wall sconces with candles also set the right mood. Avoid artificial light unless it has a dimmer; any bulb set on more than the lowest level will be too bright. Torches are essential for garden parties. And illuminating the walkway to your home will create an aura of sensual anticipation.

For music, one can never go wrong with jazz. Not fusion – choose music from the 1930s and 1940s, even if it was recorded by contemporary jazz players. A mixture of vocal and instrumental pieces will work best. Classical music, such as Eric Satie or Chopin, can also fill in pockets of silence and soften the mood. And unless you are partying in your parents' basement or are hosting a record company party, avoid at all costs rap, heavy metal, country and industrial techno music. Opera, despite its highbrow appeal, is difficult to talk over and gives the appearance of a host who is trying too hard to impress.

PERSONAL PREPARATION

It is wise to be dressed and ready to greet guests at least fifteen minutes before you're expecting first arrivals. Remove any apron, put down your cooking tools and open the first bottle of red wine. Light the candles and turn on the music and let the fun begin.

When guests arrive, take their coats and get them drinks immediately. Introduce them to guests who are already there. If you're hosting solo, don't be afraid to make use of guests. Keeping people busy puts everyone at ease, so don't be shy about asking Bingo to mix up another batch of Manhattans while you check on the first course.

And make the cocktail hour an hour: always ensure that dinner is served at a reasonable time. Feeding people when they're drunk and tired is the most frequent mistake among novice entertainers.

TABLE SETTING

Informal dinner party

Although the arrangement of cutlery and glasses on the table is not critical to d.p. success, there are some rules that are logical (except if you are left-handed, in which case convention kind of leaves you out of the loop) and easy to follow. Consider what you are serving and only put out what your guests will need. There's nothing worse than the feeling that you're going to knock something over because a hostess has jammed the table so full. Also, think about how the food is going to end up on the table. If you intend to plate the dinners in the kitchen, don't set dinner plates out in advance. What should be on the table in advance is this: the tablecloth (always nicer and more finished in feeling than place mats), napkins, candles, cutlery, wine and water glasses, salt and pepper and perhaps flowers (but only if they are low enough to see over from a seated position).

Positioning: when setting cutlery, think from the outside in. So if you intend to serve a meal of soup, followed by steak and salad, finished by apple tart, your table would have a steak knife on the inside right with a soup spoon to the right of the knife. On the left would be a single fork for the main course. If salad had been the first course, a second, smaller fork would have been laid on the far left. You could put a small dessert fork and spoon (and it's nice to offer people both) above the plate's spot but perpendicular to the other cutlery. Or you might simply bring dessert cutlery to the table when you serve this course.

The napkin is typically placed under the knife-side setting.

Glasses sit above the knife. Bread and butter plates sit to the left of the dinner plate.

As each course is finished, clear everything away that is no longer necessary.

Formal dining

Fish, starter and dinner forks are ranked in order of courses from the outside in on the left of the plate. On the right side of the plate, from the outside in, are the soup spoon, fish knife and dinner knife. A knife rest can be used to elevate the tip of the main course knife. The dessert spoon and fork are above the plate. Bread is served on a smaller plate to the left of the main setting with its own butter knife. Salad can be served either before or after the main course and its plate is to the right beside the soup spoon. If soup is served at the table, the soup bowl is set above the dinner plate with its own dish for spillage.

Glasses progress by size from left to right, starting with the water goblet, red wine, white wine, and finally, dessert wine. In formal settings, the napkin is placed to the left of the forks.

FOOD

First of all, remember that food is the least important element in a dinner party. That's right. In fact, nothing is more tedious than the host who makes you endure a long lecture on the grape regions of southern France and his own culinary technique. To get past your epicurial anxiety, choose simple food that doesn't require a lot of attention, such as coq au vin, which can be made in one pot earlier in the day. And practise making three or four dishes that you can become good at preparing.

Far worse than an inexperienced chef is a host who abandons her guests while she is fussing in the kitchen and then starves them until 11 p.m.

Put out finger food before guests arrive: you can never go wrong with antipasto, cheese and fruit.

SEATING

For a group of five or fewer, let people choose their own seats. Of course, ensure that your own seat is closest to the door or the stove.

If the party is of six or more, tell people where to sit. This means thinking about it in advance. (If you haven't, fake it: tell people where to sit off the top of your head). Do alternate men and women when possible. Never mind what their persuasions are; it's just better to break people up this way. Do split up couples. Couples eat plenty of meals together and have lots of opportunity for conversation. And ultimately couples prefer this as it gives them something to talk about on the way home. Place cards are a graceful touch that will save fussing at the last moment and they're elegant and old-worldly. This rather formal gesture – the seating arrangement – makes people feel cared-for and special. You've planned their night for them, and you've decided that Bingo would be fascinated by Fifi's recent trip to Guam.

CONVERSATION

As either a guest or a hostess you have a responsibility to make conversation with your neighbours to your right and left. (Those who are too shy to manage this task should accept more low-key social invitations.) If the table is small enough, the point may be moot, as a group discussion may evolve, which is best. Traditionally, at the halfway mark, the hostess would 'turn the table', simply turning from the gentleman on her left and beginning a new conversation with the man on her right. This would start a chain reaction whereby the entire table would turn their attention in the new direction. While nothing this official is currently in practice, one still must be sure to have conversation with both 'partners'.

If she finds herself next to a dud – and it does happen – an FG does her best to float the conversation. Imagine yourself as a reporter and go into interview mode. Almost everyone enjoys talking about themselves and given the opportunity, they will. Once several efforts have been made to loosen up a reticent partner, you may feel you've done your best and engage your other companions.

Do not be afraid of arguments at the dinner table: debates make for exciting dinners. However, if a debate goes on too long and you sense that other guests are becoming un-comfortable or, worse, unamused and silent, then it is time to intervene. It is your party and your house. You must change

the subject, forcibly if required, but you must do it. Lock
eyes with one of the offenders and in a loud but upbeat voice,
say, 'Thank you both for your expert opinions' and divert
your attention to another guest not involved in the fray:
'Nancy, what were you telling me about those bathroom
renovations?' And if Nancy is a true sport (i.e. an FG) she
will pick up your baton and run with it.

MAKING REQUESTS

You can no more ask for an adjustment to the guest list than
you can for a rethinking of the menu. Unless the offender has
actually swatted you across the face with his leather glove
(figuratively or literally), there is no adequate reason not to
tolerate his proximity to you. Simply offer him a polite *'enchantée'*
and move on to the more enchanting people at the gathering.

THE DINNER PARTY POST-MORTEM

It is particularly gratifying to receive a post-mortem phone
call if you are single, because you don't have a spouse to pick
over the evening with after the guests leave. Your friend is
actually doing you a service by giving you a chance to analyse
how your experiment with filo pastry went and whether the
two singletons you seated together hit it off. And if something even slightly outrageous occurred – an inappropriate
hand on a knee, loudly conveyed opinions on Islamic banking – it's not terribly naughty to have a laugh about it. Of
course, if your friend is truly mean-spirited in her remarks,
you must gently curb her habit. All but the most boorish will
get the hint if after making a nasty crack about a fellow guest,
you counter with, 'Oh, Vladimir may have a bizarre sense of
colour combination, but he is such a great guy. You know, he
said the nicest thing about you...'

The Cocktail Party

Traditionally a cocktail party is a short pre-dinner affair at which guests enjoy one or two drinks before moving on to the next phase of their evening. Today a cocktail party can mean any evening gathering at which people are dressed up and dinner is not served. A group of friends hanging out on your balcony drinking beer in the afternoon, although a pleasant activity, is not a c.p. Simply put, if no-one's in heels, it's not a cocktail party.

You might try – although it rarely works – to put firm hours on your invitation, say, 6 p.m. to 8 p.m. Better to tell guests that you have dinner reservations at 8.30. Otherwise they'll never leave and will get too drunk.

The key to cocktail party success is having a critical mass of people as soon as the party begins and getting a drink in everyone's hand immediately. As to the first point, rally your closest friends to be on time, but still expect that even they will arrive a half-hour late. As to the latter, plan your drinks carefully. If you're hostessing solo, you may want to give your guests very few options, perhaps wine which is easily poured by yourself or some helpful pal. Or martinis, which you can make in large batches (practise this first).

If you can afford to employ a waiter for your party, then go ahead and have a full bar. It's still nice, though, to have a drink that's special for that night, like champagne cocktails or Greyhounds. Resist the temptation to get too fussy with drinks – either in ingredients or appearance – they're good for a laugh but not really for drinking. And once you're out of college, there's no excuse for serving or drinking cocktails with jokey names: Orgasms, Strip and Go Naked, Sex on the Beach. Really.

Serve some kind of food whenever you're serving alcohol. Salty is better than sweet. It just tastes right and it makes people want to drink more. Plan hors d'oeuvres that can be picked up easily and consumed in one or two bites.

Offer napkins and leave them where you have laid out food. Leave empty plates or dishes for olive stones and discarded satay sticks.

Encourage movement in the room. Grab Fifi and pull her out of the conversation she's been in for twenty minutes to meet your cousin Fritz, just returned from Gstaad.

Parties on a shoestring

As we have mentioned before, it is the effort that is rewarded not its price. There is no reason that an FG on a budget cannot entertain her friends, be it a girls' night renting videos or a small cocktail party.

In fact a cocktail party is one occasion to which guests may bring their drinks, wine or what have you, and all you need to serve is finger food. Of course there are also dinners with friends to which everyone brings a course or dish and then the onus or cost isn't entirely on the hostess. Chances are that your friends know your situation and are likely in similar straits; no-one will criticize an FG for low-cost dining. They will only remember the fab time they had in her company.

Pre-party

Before the guests arrive, eat something substantial, even if you're not hungry. You won't eat any hors d'oeuvres yourself, even though you think you will. And it's important not to get too drunk too early as hostess. Alternate alcoholic drinks with mineral water. You can't do your job if you're wasted.

Accidents and Other Fiascos

If accidents happen – a glass crashes to the floor, red wine is spilled on your sofa – quickly do your best to tidy up the mess and be done with it. The glass-breaker will feel bad enough without you crying that it was your favourite whatever. Assure them that nothing could matter less to you and make light of it. Most of all, don't dwell on it.

Despite the civil nature of the Fabulous Girl, there will be occasions when events will rattle her. One such occurrence may be the uninvited guest. You've carefully planned your dinner for six down to the last toothpick when in walks guest number six with three pals he ran into on his way over. Unfortunately you cannot ask them to leave; you must, in fact, feed them and be civil at all costs. It may mean, however, that your serving portions will shrink substantially.

At a more free-flowing gathering such as a cocktail party or barbecue, unwelcome guests may 'crash' your party. An ex-lover perhaps? With his new girlfriend? Once again the FG allows her graciousness to guide her. Smile and greet them warmly, then ignore them for the rest of the evening. Some people do have a nerve.

If after all your practice you still burn dinner and it is inedible, don't despair. Call and order in. One can never go wrong with Thai food; it's relatively inexpensive and it's more exotic than Chinese. But most of all, don't make a big drama of it. Laugh it off – is is rather funny, isn't it?

OTHER PEOPLE'S FIGHTS

It's one thing to have a heated debate over the *filet mignon*. It's quite another to have couple number one engage in a major fight in front of the other guests. No-one wants to witness other people's relationships at such a raw level. If someone is crying and another yelling or storming away from the table, then you must break decorum and direct the offenders to behave themselves or to leave your home. If the lout is stewing at the table while his girlfriend is sobbing on the sofa, remark pointedly, 'Don't you think you should go to her?' When he does, resume your conversation with the other guests and ignore the event. When the crazy-in-love couple leave, you will all have plenty to dish about.

Dress Codes

Make them. Letting people know what is expected of them puts them at ease. Dress codes spare your friends the embarrassment of showing up to your dressy cocktail party in jeans. If you are sending printed invitations, the dress code goes on it. And please, God, deliver us from 'creative black tie', which means exactly nothing and only serves to drive men into great-than-normal states of anxiety. If your invitations are delivered over the phone or by e-mail, also include the dress code, as in, 'Please come to our place for smart cocktails on Friday night' or 'Come by for a casual barbecue on Sunday'.

Parties of any sort are better when people dress up. (And when we say dress up, we don't mean only formal, just that some effort has been made toward an attractive appearance.) Not only is a room lovelier full of well-turned-out people, but it adds to the feeling of festiveness. It's an event – even if a small one – not just the coincidence of more than three people in a room.

Even at a low-key event, you can make an effort. You must consider your appearance to be part of your contribution to the evening (or afternoon). Of course as the hostess, this is doubly important. Your attractive, kempt appearance is a measure of your appreciation for your guests.

The End

It's perfectly fine – at a c.p. – to announce last call for drinks in order to let people know it's nearly time to go, but only if you stated the end time in your invitation.

At a later party or at a successful d.p. where people are lingering, it's fine to kick people out if it's a week night and it's midnight, or if it's past 1.30 a.m. any night at all. 'OK, gang, it's a school night and I've got to get to bed' is not rude. People would rather be told this than realize the next day that you were dying to get them out of your place for the last hour of the evening.

The Gracious Guest

The FG is always the perfect guest at any type of function. She always remembers to bring the hostess a gift. The best choice is a bottle of wine, especially if she has sought out the menu and has chosen a wine that is complementary.

Flowers, while a lovely thought, are actually quite inconvenient, because the host or hostess has to find a vase, cut the flowers and arrange them all while greeting other guests. If flowers are her choice of gift, the FG will have them delivered ahead of time.

Offer to help the host in any way that seems suitable, be it in preparation or in clean-up. We're not suggesting that you snap on the rubber gloves and wash the dishes, but carrying in a few plates is never unappreciated.

Perhaps most importantly, be in tune to your inner party

clock. Know when it's time to leave. If you're the last person there, it's time to go home. Likewise, if you know the host wants guests to leave and you see that certain people are going to linger and outstay their welcome, then subtly hint that 'we're going to all turn into pumpkins soon' and encourage others to leave with you.

Dealing with the Press at Your Parties

There are very few times when 'off the record' means anything these days. People who either work in the media or are famous for any reason need to define their own understanding of when things are on or off the record. If you and/or your friends are members of the press (or otherwise famous), it should be understood that when you are socializing either at home or at a bar, it's off-the-record time. You will quickly become a social pariah if you break this rule yourself, and you don't want your parties to be known as events where those in attendance break this rule. Anyone who makes hay out of a 'friend's' drunken confessions or, worse, calls the tabloids to leak such stories should be ostracized.

Of course if you're working on a magazine article about Yves Saint Laurent's contribution to fashion and you happen to meet his muse Loulou de la Falaise while she is recounting her holiday with the designer, by all means ask her discreetly if she would talk on the record with you. If she declines, you must graciously accept that.

Six months went by and I attended many dinner parties. Everyone else seemed to get it together. Then one day N.G. asked me, 'Why don't we host a dinner party together? We owe so many people.'

'Great, I'll call the caterers,' I scoffed.

'*We'll* host the party. No more of this *me me me* selfishness,' he joked.

It all started again, like some disastrous déjà vu dinner. Only N.G. and I began to prepare the food hours ahead of time. We opted for simplicity: mixed green salad with goat's cheese and balsamic vinaigrette, beef burgundy with roasted rosemary new potatoes. I had just finished putting out the starters when the first guests arrived: Eleanor and Missy with Joe and a couple of N.G.'s friends.

Inside I was quaking with the memories of the last dinner party, but somehow I, er, we pulled it off. The candles, the starters, the wine, the music and no children. N.G. was a gracious host and I was a fabulous hostess.

Everyone had a good time, dinner was fab, the conversation was fab. We rocked.

Eleanor and Missy were the last to leave. While they were putting on their coats, I said to Eleanor, 'Here, you might as well take back that bottle of Scotch. We never opened it and I won't drink it.'

'Are you sure?'

'Positive, and thanks for bringing it.'

As they left, I could sense Missy was disapproving of something.

N.G. and I decided clean-up could wait till the morning.

Fabulous Girl Epilogue

There are a few truths in life that the Fabulous Girl must embrace to satisfy her goals and attain happiness.

LEARN THE WORD 'NO'

This may appear simple, but for many young women it is the hardest word to speak aloud. Most FGs were raised by their parents and by society to be 'nice girls'. This creates in them an undying desire to be popular, which often translates into trying too hard to be liked. There will be times when an FG is invited to a party, asked to babysit or asked out by a man in whom she just has no interest. But, she feels obliged to say yes because what if that person hates her for saying no? Likewise, if she's swamped in her own job and a colleague wants to leave early or switch shifts, then the FG says yes to be nice, because she doesn't want anyone to think she's a bitch.

But saying no doesn't mean that you are a snob, or that you will lose friends or work. It means you are in control of your life. If every Sunday at 10 a.m. you go to yoga but your new, groovy friends want you to go shopping with them, you should not fear that the groovy girls will never invite you out again. Don't accept another freelance assignment when you can't possibly work any harder out of fear that the editor will never call on you again. He or she will; the fact that you are busy shows you are good and in demand, not that you are a loser. So practise the word 'no' in front of a mirror or when you are driving your car; once you learn to say it out loud it will get easier and so will your life.

LEARN TO SAY 'YES'

The flip side of the nice-girl condition is caution. You want to do everything right, so you don't do anything at all. At least that way you're not making any mistakes, right? Forget it. You've got to be willing to take risks in life. Move to a different city. Apply for a job you're not quite qualified for. Doing something for the first time is frightening because it can make you feel stupid, but that's about the worst of it. And no-one has ever become perfect at something the first time they tried it. As one FG was heard to declare, the person who sits at her desk and does the work gets to write the book, not the person who thought about doing it. It's simple but true.

TAKING RESPONSIBILITY

Even an FG makes mistakes in her work or behaviour. Admit it. There is nothing less gracious than passing the blame onto someone else. It does not befit an FG to whine excuses to anyone. A simple 'I was wrong, my mistake, I'm sorry' is sufficient, and it's much more disarming and easy to accept than a lengthy diatribe. This is vital socially. You have a friend you've been ignoring, she had a major event in her life, you forget to return her calls. Months go by, and as time passes your guilt makes it seem impossible ever to call her again. What do you do? Telephone the very next time you think of her. She may be hostile, but all you can do is say, 'Sorry, I've been so busy lately. There is no excuse though, I've been a bad friend' and go from there. You'll find that most people can't continue being angry with someone who admits their own guilt.

THEY'RE NOT TALKING ABOUT YOU

When you're making big or small decisions about your life, it's easy to slip into the habit of viewing your life as if from the outside. What will it look like if I don't go through with that plan I talked about for six months? What will my neighbour think if I don't make it to her car boot sale? Who will ever forget the fool I made of myself at the Christmas party? The fact is that most people are self-absorbed and aren't thinking about you at all. And we mean that in the best way. No-one is sitting around thinking, 'Why did she do that?' They are thinking about their own troubles and their own embarrassments. And if you do find yourself in the undesirable position of being the topic of gossip, while this is uncomfortable, it will absolutely pass. If people do bother to fixate on someone else's life, it is almost always short-lived. Console yourself with knowing that gossip is only fun when it's fresh. Someone else will be the target soon enough.

KINDNESS AND EMPATHY

Walk a mile in someone else's Manolos and...well, you get the drift. Always try to see the other side of a story, even if you despise the other side of the story, and life will get easier.

ANGER AND JEALOUSY

Anger and jealousy are high-maintenance emotions. Far too much energy is wasted by remaining angry at someone or about something. Resolve what went wrong, vow not to let it happen again and move on. There is so much more to do in life. Jealousy zaps an FG's strength; while a little bit is natural, if it's ruling your world, then it's time to regroup and do something that empowers you to get over it. Like therapy – frankly, we cannot imagine a life that doesn't need a good shrinking once in a while.

HUMOUR

Life is nothing else if not funny. There is always a humorous side to events and situations. An FG finds it and laughs. It may take hours, days or weeks to be found, but that humour is there. It may sound coy, but sometimes recounting your disastrous day with a humorous exaggeration of its tragedies to a sympathetic friend can entertain both of you. Sometimes an FG just needs to picture her life as her own movie and that will be enough to lighten the burden. What would happen next? A well-placed witty line is also a gem during intense moments.

PATIENCE

The world is a crazy, hectic place. But where else can you go? The Fabulous Girl understands that little things can irritate her. She knows, however, that annoying spots like supermarket checkouts, crowded tubes, clogged roads and clearance sales are also just silly. An FG will take a deep breath and remember that an extra ten minutes isn't going to destroy her life and she will simply smile at the chaos around her. It may even happen that her bemused calm in these irritating scenes will be a gentle guide to others.

THE SIX-MONTHS RULE

A relative of the patience rule, it is simply this: when down and out, or stressed or blue, an FG will imagine her life six months into the future: will this current dilemma matter at all? Will her life be catastrophically affected? If the answer is that the FG won't give a hoot, then she doesn't need to be so concerned in the moment of seeming crisis. Again, take that deep breath and smile: this too shall pass. Very few things in life are worth the agony of lost sleep or anxiety attacks.

THE ROLLER-COASTER RIDE

One of the most important life lessons an FG should learn is that her life will never be all fabulous or all horrible. It will be fabulous and horrible – up and down, all the time, till the day she dies. An FG learns that if she's riding a wave to good things, she needn't feel guilty or fear the sky's falling, or if something bad occurs, that she's being punished. It doesn't work that way. No-one is keeping points. Instead just go with it and be confident that when life is shaky, some sort of stabilizer is around the corner to set things in balance. An FG takes control to ensure that balance is met and does not rely solely on fate to change things. Armed with her charm, wit, style and manners, she can ride the downs as graciously as the ups. She's a Fabulous Girl and she inspires others to be just as fabulous.

The next day Missy rang up Eleanor at work.

'You know I was asking a few people at work about what you did last night?'

'What are you talking about?'

'Taking back that bottle of Scotch. I hate to break it to you, El, but that was poor etiquette.'

'What? It was not.'

'I was talking about it with Joe and his mother and my colleagues here and we all agreed that it was wrong.'

Eleanor was horrified. 'You discussed this with all those people? Haven't you got anything better to do? And quite frankly you are wrong. I didn't ask for it back; it was given to me. That is completely correct etiquette.'

'Are you sure?'

'She's right,' I had to tell Missy later that day. Placating her was just too annoying. Besides, in this instance she was wrong.

'I don't know.'

'Missy, I gave Eleanor back the Scotch. She declined at first but then took it at my insistence.'

'Who knows for sure though, you know?' Missy was still indignant.

299

But I knew. In fact, it slowly dawned on me that I knew a lot about how to treat people with proper decorum. And it didn't make me a stuffy old shirt either. I was fabulous. In fact, I could write a book about it.

Acknowledgements

Thanks to our editors, Maya Mavjee and Martha Kanya-Forstner, for their brilliance, dedication and all-round Holly-ness; everyone at Transworld, especially Diana Beaumont, for embracing the Fabulous Girl; Anne McDermid, Jennifer Heyns and Kelly Dignan for making things work; Roxanna Bikadoroff for creating the Fabulous Girl exactly as we'd imagined her; Brad MacIver and Fernando Resende for helping us find Roxanna; Gabor Jurina for our picture; Stephanie Fysh for making us sound better than we are; Sara Borins for early encouragement; Katherine Ashenberg for being our decorous and delightful opponent in a Globe and Mail-fabricated etiquette stand off; our own army of FGs who have road-tested every bit of this book and more: Suzanne boyd, Lynn Creighton, Leanne Delap, Karine Ewart, Shirley Farrell, Carole Hines, Laura Keogh, Shannon Lee, Michelle Loretta, Debbie Marsh, Leah McLaren, Erin McNamara, Jane Miller, Carolynne Nelson, Jackie Nelson, Roberta Pazdro, Tralee Pearce, Elizabeth Renzettie, Martha Sharpe, Vivian Vassos and Meredyth Young; the irreplaceable FBs: Angel David, Ronald Farrell, Richard Hay, Lindsay Mahon, David Marsh, Alexander Nagel, Trevor Northeast, Doug Saunders, Scott Sellers, Arlen J. Vranic and Doug Wallace; The Globe and Mail, particularly Cathrin Bradbury, Sheree-Lee Olson and Carl Wilson for ongoing support of the 'Urban Decourm' column; Mark kingwell for his enthusiasm and excessively long-term loan of his vintage etiquette book library; Michael Stokes for generosity from Hollywood; and Russell Smith for support and love.